PORTFOLIO

GAMES INDIANS PLAY

V. RAGHUNATHAN was a professor of finance for nearly two decades, at IIM, Ahmedabad. In 2001 he joined the corporate world as president of ING Vysya Bank. At present he is a member of the top management in the GMR Group, an infrastructure major. Since 1990 he has also been a Visiting Professor at the University of Bocconi, in Milan, where his teaching interest in recent years has been behavioural finance.

Raghunathan has written over 400 academic papers and popular articles, and five books in the field of finance and investments. He also writes a regular guest column for the *Economic Times*.

Raghunathan boasts of what is probably the largest private collection of ancient locks in the country. He has also been a cartoonist briefly with a national daily, played chess at the all-India level and sketched competitively in the years gone by. To relax, he fixes mechanical clocks. He lives in India and can be contacted at v.raghunathan@gmail.com

PRAISE FOR THE BOOK

'Raghunathan tackles the peculiarities of Indianness using game theory and behavioural economics. Using everyday examples, he probes the reasons behind our conflicting tendencies'
—*Deccan Chronicle*

'Raghunathan bluntly challenges the reader to stand up to scrutiny ... He replays the fine art of unspoken "inetiquette" refined in India'
—Soumya Sitaraman in *Deccan Herald*

'An incredibly interesting read'
—*First City*

'The book takes the reader through some powerful insights into why we Indians need to introspect ...' ·
—*The Analyst*, The ICFAI University Press

Games Indians Play
Why We Are the Way We Are

V. RAGHUNATHAN

Foreword by N.R. Narayana Murthy

PORTFOLIO
PENGUIN

PORTFOLIO

Published by the Penguin Group

Penguin Books India Pvt. Ltd, 11 Community Centre, Panchsheel Park, New Delhi 110 017, India

Penguin Group (USA) Inc., 375 Hudson Street, New York, New York 10014, USA

Penguin Group (Canada), 90 Eglinton Avenue East, Suite 700, Toronto, Ontario, M4P 2Y3, Canada (a division of Pearson Penguin Canada Inc.)

Penguin Books Ltd, 80 Strand, London WC2R 0RL, England

Penguin Ireland, 25 St Stephen's Green, Dublin 2, Ireland (a division of Penguin Books Ltd)

Penguin Group (Australia), 707 Collins Street, Melbourne, Victoria 3008, Australia (a division of Pearson Australia Group Pty Ltd)

Penguin Group (NZ), 67 Apollo Drive, Rosedale, Auckland 0632, New Zealand (a division of Pearson New Zealand Ltd)

Penguin Group (South Africa) (Pty) Ltd, Block D, Rosebank Office Park, 181 Jan Smuts Avenue, Parktown North, Johannesburg 2193, South Africa

Penguin Books Ltd, Registered Offices: 80 Strand, London WC2R 0RL, England

First published in Portfolio by Penguin Books India 2006
This paperback edition published in 2007

Copyright © V. Raghunathan 2006
Foreword copyright © N.R. Narayana Murthy 2006

All rights reserved

18 17 16 15 14 13 12

ISBN 9780143063117

The views and opinions expressed in this book are the author's own and the facts are as reported by him which have been verified to the extent possible, and the publishers are not in any way liable for the same.

Typeset in Minion by R. Ajith Kumar, New Delhi
Printed at Repro India Ltd., Navi Mumbai

Contents

FOREWORD **vii**
N.R. Narayana Murthy

PREFACE **xi**

PROLOGUE **1**

WHY ARE WE THE WAY WE ARE? **6**

ON INTELLIGENCE AND RATIONALITY **22**

SIMPLE PRISONER'S DILEMMA AND WE THE
SQUEALERS! **32**

ITERATIVE PRISONER'S DILEMMA AND THE
GENTLEMAN STRATEGY **49**

CAN COMPETITION LEAD TO COOPERATION? **66**

SELF-REGULATION, FAIRNESS AND US **75**

ARE WE THE WORLD'S BIGGEST FREE RIDERS? **105**

SYSTEMIC CHAOS **115**

THE VEERAPPAN DILEMMA: THE POSER
ANSWERED **132**

GAME THEORY AND THE GITA **140**

EPILOGUE **149**

APPENDIX **157**

ENDNOTES **164**

INDEX **168**

Foreword

N.R. Narayana Murthy

Games Indians Play, Dr Raghunathan's new book, is timely, and is an absorbing, illuminating study of the life and behaviour of Indians in the public sphere. It presents an economist's view on what it means to be an Indian today. I consider it a pleasure and a privilege to write the foreword for this book.

India is, now, sixty years as a free country. Yet, today, many of the goals set during the time of India's independence have not been realized. Our country faces multiple, urgent challenges of poverty, corruption and emerging social crises in health, education and population growth. Twenty six per cent of Indians remain below the poverty line, and 39 per cent of the country is illiterate. Public infrastructure in India remains either weak or non-existent—a large segment of India's population lacks access to the most basic resources. Over one-third of Indians lack access to clean water or proper sanitation facilities, and 30 per cent of the Indian population remains unconnected by a proper road. Corruption is pervasive in India's institutions—close to one per cent of the country's GDP today is lost to bribes alone.

In his book, Raghunathan takes a novel perspective on India's myriad economic and social challenges. He asserts that, while the resources to address India's problems are available, serious problems persist due to apathy and a 'lack of public conscience' among the Indian population. This, he notes, holds true for Indians across all walks of life—be it the political field, the bureaucracy, the business sector or the salaried and working class.

Raghunathan examines Indian social behaviour through game theory and behavioral economics, and he relies particularly on the work of game theorists such as John von Neumann, Oskar Morgenstern and John Nash. For example, he uses the principle of prisoner's dilemma to analyse the benefit of selfish versus cooperative strategies among individuals and to discuss the lack of concern among Indians for public infrastructure and facilities. Raghunathan points out that Indians view their fellow citizens—including the authorities—as apathetic (or 'selfish') towards public infrastructure, and consequently see maximum benefit in being apathetic as well. The 'cooperative strategy' of maintaining infrastructure for good public use becomes increasingly unprofitable, as more and more people are seen as selfish. In such an environment, all people eventually pursue 'selfish strategies', and pursue routes that maximize personal gain at the expense of public good. Such an attitude has led, in the long term, to the present situation of public apathy for law and order, the fractured sense of public good and corruption across all sections of Indian society.

Raghunathan gives us a strong appreciation of how and why Indians have cultivated behaviours that are so destructive to the fabric of the larger community. His book is filled with revealing insights on how our social attitudes impact our ability to address the economic and social challenges that face the country. Raghunathan's writing is humorous and filled with anecdotes that are both amusing and thought-provoking. For instance, he notes the irony of having to pay a bribe in order to pay land registration fees in India, essentially paying a bribe to give money to the government! However, this has become so commonplace that most Indians no longer think twice about making the payment.

India, thanks to its emerging economic and demographic advantages, has the opportunity to grow into a developed, prosperous economy over the next two decades. However, to enable growth that is both sustainable and equitable, Indians have to recognize the challenges we face as a society, and address them with courage and a commitment towards reform. A stronger understanding of ourselves and of our social structures is essential to enable this. *Games Indians Play* is an intelligent, insightful effort in this direction.

Preface

My interest in the question 'Why are we (Indians) the way we are?' originated in Italy—in the lovely city of Milan, to be precise. The question kept popping up in my mind as I started teaching an elective course on game theory and behavioural economics at SDA Bocconi, in their Master's in International Economics and Management Programme. While preparing for the course, I went back to a splendid series of articles by Douglas R. Hofstadter in the *Scientific American* that I had read in the 1980s. In fact it was one of Hofstadter's wonderfully written essays on prisoner's dilemma that had first awakened my interest in game theory, which in due course led me to behavioural economics, and later into using this framework to look into the Indianness of us Indians. While I did attain some nodding familiarity with the works of true game theorists such as John von Neumann, John Nash and others, to me they came after Hofstadter. I would forever have remained innocent of their works, or at any rate would not have got as interested in their works as I subsequently did, had it not been for Hofstadter's easy and highly readable interpretation of game theory.

Over the years, the prisoner's dilemma framework helped me understand a wee bit better the characteristics of human rationality, irrationality, egotism, selfishness, antagonism, competition, collaboration and cooperation among us Indians vis-à-vis the rest of the world in countless day-to-day situations.

In addition, the works of Daniel Kahneman, Amos Tversky, Richard Thaler and many others who developed the whole new field of behavioural economics in the last twenty-five years or so have also helped me get some degree of understanding of ourselves as a people. I have used the material of many of these illustrious researchers and scientists in preparing a window through which to view our Indianness.

I am eternally thankful to them all for the insights they have provided me into human behaviour.

In writing this book, occasionally I have borrowed from a few of my own writings from a monthly guest column that I write for the *Economic Times*. I thank the *ET* for their indulgence in allowing me the liberty.

Krishan Chopra, the highly exacting executive editor of Penguin India, has been the biggest value-adder to this book, with his incisive, aggressive comments on draft after draft. Equally valuable has been the contribution of my copy editor, who helped transform a rather flippantly written manuscript into a book in its present form. She has had a hard job—believe me. Meena, my best friend and also incidentally my wife, has edited the manuscript at every stage and in doing so has helped improve the book substantially. Shweta Parekh, another very dear friend of mine, made some useful and critical suggestions after going through the first draft of the book. I have incorporated many of them. Mr M.P.V. Shenoi—a friend of my late parents, and now mine—gave valuable comments in the early stages of the book; Pramod Nair, my erstwhile executive assistant and my very dear friend as well, was, as ever, extravagantly encouraging with his comments on some of the draft chapters; Samir Barua, my friend of twenty-five years from IIM, Ahmedabad, helped me clarify a problem involving probability theory, while dealing with the 'Luring Lottery'. Stuthi Shetty, another close friend, gave me her legal advice on a few chapters; and Saee, my former student from IIM, Ahmedabad (1994–96), and now a good friend, made incisive comments on some of my early chapters, which helped me clarify how I wanted the book to progress. Manish Sabharwal, my neighbour and a very good friend—among the best-read persons I know—was the source of the latest books on behavioural economics. But for him my fund of reading would have been substantially poorer. And Sudhir Kamath, my batchmate and pal since our doctoral days, not only gave me encouraging feedback on the initial chapters but also supplied some very apt anecdotes on dilemmas for inclusion in the book. And finally, Mamata Pandya, a great friend of my wife's, and through her mine as well, did that final reading of the manuscript, and corrected many of those little errors that invariably slip in.

It's touching how much good friends do for you, especially in India. I am deeply grateful to them all (with the usual disclaimers with regard to shortcomings of the book!).

In the book, I have settled for 'he', 'him' etc. for the third person rather than 'she' and 'her', though I think I am reasonably gender sensitive. I find the use of the feminine form somewhat contrived; the use of he/she or him/her rather stretched; and the use of plural, as in 'they' and 'their', not always user-friendly.

My father-in-law, Dr A. Nagarathnam, an outstanding scientist and scholar, has always helped me with editing the manuscripts of my books. With some 300 scientific papers to his credit, his value addition to a manuscript was always significant. This time too, he was enthusiastically looking forward to working on my manuscript. In fact, so was I. Unfortunately, around February 2005, he met with an accident, resulting in a head injury, and passed away towards the end of 2005, after having been completely bedridden for nearly nine months, with only occasional snatches of consciousness. It would forever be my regret not to have had his comments on the book. My hunch is he, with his British English, may not have quite approved of my somewhat relaxed language. I know the book has lost much for lack of the benefit of his inputs.

Appa, I dedicate this book to you.

Prologue

Notorious forest brigand Veerappan was shot dead
by Tamil Nadu Special Task Force late tonight in
the Hogenekal forest area in Dharmapuri district.

Tribune, 18 October 2004

THE VEERAPPAN DILEMMA

I think Veerappan was a big-time robbing-hood even by Indian
standards, where such hoods abound at all times, in all forms
and at all places. Quite probably he is listed in the *Limca Book
of Records* for carrying the highest-ever prize (Rs 50 crore) on
his head announced by a single state government of India. For
most of us, that is serious money. So I wasn't surprised to read
in the *Times of India* one morning (20 November 2004) that
'cooks, cleaners, dhobis, current STF [special task force] men,
Chamrajnagar District Police, Mysore District Police . . . from
those who served the STF many years ago in minor capacities
to policemen who served in the districts on fringe [sic] of what
was once called Veerappan country' and the pussy cats, poodles
and parrots of all those mentioned have all been staking claim
to the award.

As I write this prologue, the number of claimants is already close to 850 and still climbing. And why not, with such booty available for the asking?

The news item has inspired me to present you a poser. I have adapted it from Douglas Hofstadter's treatment of 'Luring Lottery'.[1]

Suppose the Karnataka chief minister is in a quandary about whom to give or not give the award, given the stampede under way to claim it. He is afraid that if he does not take a decision one way or the other, it may not be long before half the country stakes claim for its role in leading Veerappan to his death. The chief minister has one more problem. While he has announced the reward of Rs 50 crore in a moment of bravado, vying with the Tamil Nadu chief minister, he is not sure his state coffer has that much loose change. With all this in mind, and the help of his clever additional chief secretary, he has devised a special scheme to give away the award. He has decided that the entire sum must go to a single individual.

His home department has shortlisted twenty names from the list of claimants with the same transparency with which petrol pumps, cooking gas agencies, plum land plots, etc. are usually allotted by any babu in a state government. Each of these twenty is assumed to be highly intelligent; or else they would not have survived squealing on Veerappan. To each of these, the section officer in the chief minister's secretariat writes:

Dear So and So

I am hereby directed by the Hon'ble Chief Minister to write to you to state that you are among the final 20 chosen to receive Rs 50 crore as a reward for your vital role in leading Sri Munusamy Veerappan into the ambush laid out by our brave STF men, under the leadership of our beloved Chief Minister.

The benevolent self of Hon'ble CM had very kindly announced an award of Rs 50 crore to anyone who helped catch the brigand, dead or alive. Hon'ble CM is a man of his words. He has shown the rare resolve to keep his words by ensuring that only one individual will qualify to receive the award.

Accordingly, I am hereby directed to congratulate you and state that if you are desirous of receiving the award of Rs 50 crore, you should write to the undersigned and see that it reaches before the close of working hours of this Friday (5 p.m.), stating (in triplicate):

Your Address

Yes, I would like to receive the award of Rs 50 crore only (Rupees Fifty Crore Only) for the valiant role I played in bringing about the fatal encounter with Sri Munusamy Veerappan.

Yours Faithfully

Signature

Your Name:
Date:

Important Terms & Conditions: Kindly note that certain strict terms and conditions apply. You must read the following very carefully and comply:

i.   You are one of the 20 brave citizens shortlisted for the award. An identical letter is being sent to the other 19, whose identity is withheld from you.

ii. You will become eligible for the entire award, provided your communication in triplicate is received by the undersigned before the close of working hours this Friday, and also provided yours is the ONLY communication that the CM's office receives. Should the office receive a similar communication from more than one of the 20 shortlisted candidates, nobody shall qualify to receive the award.

iii. Any attempt on your part, direct or indirect, to locate, identify or establish contact, orally or in writing or in any other form, with any of those 19 others for whatever reason will immediately and summarily disqualify you from receiving the award, and the decision of the CM's office in this regard shall be final and binding. You will be watched carefully from now until the due date for the communication (coming Friday), in order to ensure that you do not violate this important condition.

iv. It may be reiterated, as directed, that if you do not send in your communication (in triplicate), you will not be eligible to receive the award.

Now the question is would you write to the chief minister's office to claim your reward or not?

Obviously you would not want to miss your chance of getting Rs 50 crore. So you argue: 'If I don't write to the chief minister's office, there goes my 50 crore (according to clause iv). So my only option is to write that note in triplicate.'

Chances are that the other nineteen have similar thoughts. In all likelihood, the chief minister's secretariat would have all twenty letters confirming the shortlisted candidates' desire to receive the award, in quadruplicate (an extra copy added for good measure), long before the last date is reached. So there goes your reward and that of the other nineteen claimants.

Of course, as a true Indian, you are tempted to get in touch with the other nineteen on the sly, in the hope you can forge a deal with them so that only one of you writes and then everyone shares the booty equally. But the shrewd chief minister, himself a true Indian, has anticipated that and taken adequate measures to prevent you from trying to do so. He didn't become your chief minister for nothing!

Now do you see any realistic chance of you or any of the other nineteen claimants getting that award of Rs 50 crore?

CHAPTER 1

Why Are We the Way We Are?

A Manipuri girl's throat was slit allegedly by an insane man at the Gateway of India on Saturday evening. Tourist Nga Kuimi Raleng (23) died on the spot. The crowd there watched in silence as the chopper-wielding killer attacked the tourist's friend Leisha Choan (20) . . .

Express New Service, 14 August 2005

NOT WHO BUT WHY

'Who am I?' is not a question that occupies me much. I have neither the intellectual curiosity nor the intellectual endowment to ask or answer that question. But, off and on, like when I have just returned from a visit abroad (by 'abroad' I mean not only countries like the USA and the UAE but also those like the Philippines, Malaysia and Indonesia, or Botswana, Burkina Faso and Burundi), I find myself asking some less philosophical questions. For example:

Why is my sense of public hygiene so porcine? Why do I throw my garbage around with the gay abandon of an inebriated uncle flinging 500-rupee notes at a Punjabi wedding? Why do I spit with a free will, as if without that one right I would be a citizen of a lesser democracy? Why do I tear off a page from a library book, or write my name on the Taj Mahal? Why do I light a match to a football stadium, a city bus or any other handy public property, or toot my horn in a residential locality at 3 a.m.? Why do I leave a public toilet smelling even though I would like to find it squeaky clean as I enter it? Why don't I contribute in any way to help maintain a beautiful public park? Why is my concern for quality in whatever I do rather Lilliputian? Why is my ambition or satisfaction threshold at the level of a centipede's belly button? Why do I run the tap full blast while shaving even when I know of the acute water shortage in the city? Why don't I stop or slow down my car to allow a senior citizen or a child to cross the road? Why do I routinely jump out of my seat in a mad rush for the overhead baggage even before the aircraft comes to a halt, despite the repeated entreaties of the cabin crew? Why do I routinely disregard an airline's announcement to board in orderly groups in accordance with seat numbers? Why does it not hurt my national pride that in international terminals abroad extra staff is appointed at gates from which flights to India are to depart? Why don't I vote? Why don't I stand up or retaliate against social ills? Why is it that every time the government announces a well-intended measure like a higher rate of interest for senior citizens I am not averse to borrowing my ageing parents' names, or the old family maid's for that matter, to save my money? Why is it that every time the government announces no tax deduction at source for small depositors I split my bank deposit into fifteen different accounts, with active connivance of the bank manager? Why do I jump red lights with the alacrity of a jackrabbit leaping ahead of a buckshot? Why do I block the left lane, when my intention is to turn right? Or vice versa? Why do I overtake from the left? Why do I drive at night in the city with the high beam on? Why do I jump queues with the zest of an Olympic heptathlon gold hopeful?

A DIGRESSION

This last act—jumping queues—I must confess I execute with particular finesse. I have honed it to a fine art. The key to jumping queues lies in not making eye contact with the guy you are jumping ahead of. I usually employ one of the two following gambits, both of which obey the 'do-not-make-eye-contact' dictum.

In one scenario, I just sidle up, very casual-like, ahead of the guy who has been waiting his turn in the queue with bovine patience, as if I simply haven't noticed what he was up to. If per chance—for they come in all shapes, sizes and sexes—the bovine turns out to be a raging bull rather than a meek cow and is rude and crude enough to bellow and stomp the floor at my cultured ruse to jump the queue, first I acknowledge his existence as if he were a fluff ball that magically materialized from under the bed. Then with elaborate courtesy and hand gesture, I usher him ahead of me, with every pore of my being all but screaming, 'Here you go sir, ahead of me. What's all the fuss about? OK, you say you are ahead of me in the queue. So be it. Don't get excited now!' And then I look around and steal a wink or smile at some of the others, like a parent embarrassed at a child's unruly behaviour. You will be surprised at how many sympathetic winks and nods you will receive in return in our blessed country because all those civilized folks realize how childish it is of him to stick up for his place in the queue. At times I even actually cut the insolent bloke down to size, particularly if I am in a queue boarding an aircraft, with a quip like, 'Oh, I didn't know your flight was leaving ahead of mine!' That leaves the bloke nowhere to hide! Of course, you must be intelligent enough to figure out the right conditions before deploying this stratagem. It usually does not work, for example, if you wear size six shoes while the cud-chewer wears twelve. But then if he were wearing size twelve, chances are you would not try jumping the queue ahead of him in the first place.

The second 'do-not-make-eye-contact' rule is like this. Here your body language assumes weight. For example, you just walk up (again very casually) and stand next to the bovine guy ahead of you in the queue, keeping your elbow gently ahead of the guy without any overt aggression, all along looking elsewhere. In fact, anywhere but at the cud-chewer, for that is the essence of the tactic. The idea is to create an impression that you are the one in the genuine queue and it is the cud-chewer who has got his mixed up! If you have the size advantage over the cud-chewer, you could always make it a 'your-word-versus-mine' kind of an affair. Also, by now you aren't alone. There are those who lined up behind you thinking you were in the genuine queue, and now the opponents are more or less evenly pitched. If you are unable to capitalize on your size, you could always yield winking and smiling, as if to say, 'Well, all in a day's work guys! What's a small setback when you have these big blokes ready to pull a dagger at the drop of a place in the queue?'

I never use these gambits abroad. Those bovines there are big as buffalos, and have no appreciation of the fact that an honest Indian can have a native craving to break a measly queue. Wait a minute; I think I am digressing more than I meant to. I was talking about some questions I ask myself every now and then.

ARE THERE ANSWERS?

I do not do any of those 'Whys' listed earlier out of a sense of depravity. It's just that I am an average Indian; to use a cliché, 'I am like that only!' And when we multiply that average Indian by a billion, the question becomes 'Why are we the way we are?'

We could simplify life by merely saying, 'We are like that only,' till you go and spoil the party by asking, 'But *why* are we like that only?' From experience I have learned it is usually a sterile exercise to try and answer that question. Even a Naipaul in his *India: A Wounded Civilization* merely describes India's many grotesque wounds; he does not attempt to unearth the reasons for the wounds. When I first read the book in the socialist era of the 1970s, I was affronted by what I thought were unkind remarks on India based on just three visits by a person who never had a role to play in shaping this country. It took nearly two decades for me to see and understand what the great Naipaul had observed in those three visits.

Nor does the eminent sociologist M.N. Srinivas provide an answer to why we are the way we are in his splendid writings and essays. I am a lesser mortal. After much deliberation and reading, I have come to the conclusion that there is no profit in asking a second-order question like 'Why are we the way we are?'

My hopes were indeed raised when I encountered a fascinating book, *The Geography of Thought: How Asians and Westerners Think Differently . . . and Why* by Richard Nisbett. While the book provides an excellent exposition on how Western and Eastern philosophies and their ways of thinking evolved historically, and exactly in what ways and why they differ as promised by the book's title, it has one problem. The Westerners in the book are primarily Europeans, Americans and the citizens of the British Commonwealth, and the Asians are principally Chinese, Japanese and Koreans.

Indians in their traits are clubbed with the Westerners! If one is inclined to agree with the author's analysis of the Westerners, one is also compelled to disagree with his implied analysis of the Indians, for the traits of the two could not be more different. For example, Nisbett observes, 'people [Westerners] believe the same rules should apply to everyone—individuals should not be singled out for special treatment because of their personal attributes or connections to important people. Justice should be blind.' But is this statement true of us Indians, who have slotted individuals along caste and feudal lines for thousands of years? Do we seriously believe that everyone should get the same treatment and justice? If the belief does exist, is it reflected in our practices? Clearly, India eludes Nisbett's analysis. So my hope of finding an answer to the question 'Why are we the way we are?' was snuffed out once I read the book in detail.

What if one dares to ask the question 'Why?' Apparent answers begin to pour in from all over in a deluge. Is it our climate? Could it be the density of our population? Or is it really our poverty? Or perhaps our national level of literacy? (Or is it illiteracy?) Many thinkers say our population, poverty and illiteracy are the effects of the way we are and not the causes of the way we are. What then are the causes? I dig into our cultural past, historical past, colonial past, religious past, sociological past, anthropological past, or just good old plain-vanilla past till I unearth the satisfying fact that in the distant past our forefathers gave 'zero' to the world, and that we were a golden sparrow before the Mughals and the English came trooping in and plucked our feathers bald, and it follows therefore that we need answer no such question. I am what I am. We are what we are.

But there are other questions that keep rearing their heads like the hood of a defensive cobra. Am I the way I am because I am genetically encoded to be like that only? Did one of my Neanderthal ancestors strike out on his own, away from his cousins' caves, vowing to create a race that in due course would lay the foundations of a country called India, which would be among the filthiest, the ugliest, the most selfish, the most apathetic and the most corrupt in the world at the dawn of the twenty-first century? I am not a genetic expert, but if that ancestor did indeed do so, there are few who would not agree that he did a darned good job of achieving his ambition. He certainly laid a strong foundation for a long-lasting Indian culture, where even today some 70 per cent (or some such absurd percentage) of us move on the wooden wheels of bullock carts, carry construction material on our heads and grain sacks on our backs, sweep and mop our homes squatting on our haunches, and defecate on the great Indian plains exactly as we did some 5000 years ago. Perhaps that is why our souls do not rebel at disparaging references to 'Hindu fatalism' and 'Hindu rate of growth', as if our Hindu gods genetically doomed us into doing things in a predetermined fatalistic way and at a predetermined modest rate of growth and change.[1] I would hasten to add here that I use the term Hindu as a proxy for the dweller of the subcontinent representing the Indus Valley in its broadest sense.

Lest I be accused of being unduly harsh on ourselves, let me furnish some statistics.[2] China recently completed the final section of the pan-Himalayan Golmud-Lhasa railway (1956 kilometres) at 5072 metres above sea level. The final section of 1142 kilometres, running across Tibet's snow-covered plateau—dubbed the roof of the world—presented some unusual difficulties. The engineers had to contend with building on a 550-kilometre frozen belt, with the snow alternately melting and freezing in summer and winter. Workers had to breathe bottled oxygen to cope with the high altitudes and there was not a single death due to this. This stretch of 1142 kilometres was completed in a mere four years.

Or consider Phase I of Shanghai's Pu Dong Airport. A four-kilometre runway, two parallel taxiways, an 800,000-square-metre apron, twenty-eight boarding bridges, 280,000 square metres of terminal building and 50,000 square metres of cargo warehouse space designed to fly twenty million passengers, 750,000 tonnes of cargo and 126,000 flights a year—all these were completed between October 1997 and September 1999.

In the same league was the completion of the world's first Transrapid Maglev Railway in Shanghai. It too was completed in less than two years. It takes a mere eight minutes for passengers on the maglev trains, with a peak speed of 430 kilometers an hour, to travel the thirty kilometres between Pu Dong International Airport and the downtown. What is more, this gave the Chinese technicians eight international patents in the manufacturing of high-tech girders.

The economic development, political integration and social pride that projects such as these engender for China and its far-flung people are all too obvious to elucidate.

Cut to India. Impressive as the completion of the Konkan Railway or the Delhi Metro Railway have been, they pale in comparison to the Chinese projects, especially where implementation skills and political will are concerned. Consider the statistics. It took seven to ten years to complete the 760-kilometre Konkan Railway. As for the Delhi Metro, between 1950 and 1990, some thirty feasibility studies were carried out by various bodies to evaluate an alternative transportation system for Delhi. The final go-ahead came in 1990. Delhi Metro Rail Corporation Limited was established in 1995 and the first phase of eleven kilometres was completed in 2004. The eighteen-kilometre Calcutta Metro took a good twenty-four years to complete, from 1971 to 1995. In Bangalore, a flyover near the airport has been three years in the making, and is still going strong because the underlying soil was found to be shifty. Our new expressways, the Golden Quadrilateral included, are perennially in a state of half-finish. One or the other side of the throughways is being laid or else under litigation at any given time. It is common for us to see a part of a road dug up one fine morning. And it is equally common to see that road in exactly the same state even after we return from our summer vacation, when in most other countries such works are carried out practically overnight. Now that is what we mean by the 'Hindu rate' of doing things.

Naipaul puts it with some finesse when he says, 'Hindu morality, centered on the self and self-realization, has its own social corruptions . . .' Is this special corruption then the answer to that 'Why'? I wish the genetic argument was the answer, for then we could wash our hands off any responsibility towards the way we are. If there is anything wrong with us, it is not our fault. We are simply like that only—genetically.

In short, I do not know if we are 'like that' for reasons of our poverty, education, population, climate, colonial past or whatever. I do not think the traits I listed earlier are the exclusive preserve of the socio-economically challenged segment of the country. Those of us breaking queues at the airports do exactly what our brothers and sisters do at a ration shop or at the public tap. Population and climate? Well, most of the Far Eastern economies have climatic conditions and population densities little different from ours, and their cities and towns are nevertheless far more clean and orderly. Colonial past? There are any number of countries outside our subcontinent that had been colonized and have bounced back as working and orderly states after suffering a much worse past than us.

WHAT THIS BOOK IS AND IS NOT ABOUT

Surely many of our behavioural traits, as evidenced by my spew of questions earlier, may also have to do with weak enforcement and weaker consequences of enforcement in our country. There could be a million other persuasive reasons for our being what we are and we could expound on these, given our ability to blather and debate anything till the cows come home. But I shall not. Because this book is not about finding external excuses for our behaviour. After all, it is we who are responsible for the enforcement and regulation of our behaviour.

If so, what is this book about? What aperture do I retain to show you a fog-free view of our Indianness you have not seen already? What are the attributes that we may say define our Indianness?

The questions raised above are many and mundane and probably need some classification. I have therefore pigeonholed these questions into twelve 'canons' of Indianness and discuss them in the course of this book. These characteristics are:
1. Low trustworthiness
2. Being privately smart and publicly dumb
3. Fatalist outlook
4. Being too intelligent for our own good
5. Abysmal sense of public hygiene

6. Lack of self-regulation and sense of fairness
7. Reluctance to penalize wrong conduct in others
8. Mistaking talk for action
9. Deep-rooted corruption and a flair for free riding
10. Inability to follow or implement systems
11. A sense of self-worth that is massaged only if we have the 'authority' to break rules
12. Propensity to look for loop holes in laws

I have not listed the characteristics in any structured order. I intend to throw some light on them in the backdrop of game theory and behavioural economics. Game theory is nothing but the economists' term for what psychologists call the theory of social situations. And behavioral economics is the interaction between psychology and economics that tries to explain how human limitations and complexities affect choice. I do not see the need to devote a separate chapter for each of the traits listed above. I will just peck, bite and nibble at them here and there, helping to wash them down with the spirit of game theory and a dash of behavioural economics. The aim is to make the reader understand how and why our current behavioural traits need to change if we wish to be counted among the more civilized people of the world. In this sense this book is not quite diagnostic. Rather, it is akin to a CAT scan that could provide a better peek into one's own self.

Many may take umbrage at my inherent proposition that we are largely a less-civilized people than most other major nationalities and hence we need to take a fresh look at ourselves. A word of advice to such readers: To consider the time taken to read this book as well spent, there are three points that the readers must be ready to acknowledge as prerequisites: one, that there is indeed something wrong with us; two, that there are aspects in our traits that do not seem to sit well in a modern civilized society; and three, that merely because other modern and civilized societies, whether occidental or oriental, also suffer from many ills, it does not make our own ills any more acceptable.

By calling our society less civilized, I do not imply that we have no strengths as a people. Of strengths we have many. We are intelligent and industrious (though perhaps in a more self-serving and less productive way than most other people), have strong family values (which are often the cause for nepotism), are friendly (even if to the point of being obsequious to the occidental skin, never having really hatched out of our colonial shell) and stick together in times of hardship, as could be seen during the sundry wars we were engaged in during the last few decades, and in the aftermath of the December 2004 tsunami.

But then, these traits are not singular to us. The Israelis, the Chinese and the Japanese are no less industrious than we are, and they are probably a little less self-serving and far more productive as individuals. The Chinese, the Japanese and the Italians have family values no less robust than ours. And the United States also showed how the entire country could come together during the 9/11 tragedy. But our failings, it would seem, are almost singular to us, or to our subcontinent maybe.

It is a fact that we are an ancient civilization and that up to the medieval times we were among the most advanced civilizations. The putrefaction of our civilization perhaps set in a good thousand years ago, from which time our contribution to the world went steadily downhill. But then, a glorious past can hardly be a consolation for a sorry present. That the Indus Valley civilization at Mohenjo-Daro and Harappa had glorious town planning over 2000 years ago is cold consolation for our wretched present-day cities, towns and villages. While other civilizations have gone on to build upon their past, we are merely living off it and, what is more, we have been doing it for over a thousand years! Now what riches in the world can withstand such an onslaught on its principal? Once again, Naipaul comes to mind: 'How often in India—at every level—rational conversation about the country's problems trails away into talk of magic, of the successful prophecies of astrologers, of the wisdom of auspicious hours, of telepathic communications, and actions taken in response to some inner voice!'[3] Is that our Freudian way of escaping harsh realities?

SOME DISCLAIMERS
Let me place before you some explicit disclaimers, warnings and cautions:

1. This is not a research-based book, even if it borrows from the researches of some, and a few of my own, not necessarily rigorous, experiments.

2. This is not a book on game theory or behavioural economics, even if it uses the two disciplines as useful crutches to precipitate some degree of analytical awareness on some of the average Indian traits that I find bothersome.

3. This is not a book on sociology, even if it attempts to address a social issue like the Indianness of us Indians.
4. Most of the conclusions arrived at are at worst conjectural and at best plausible hypotheses for further research that students of behavioural economics or social psychology, particularly those in India, may wish to test.
5. This book is not about every aspect of Indianness and it certainly does not touch upon the many achievements that we, as a country or a people, may have.

This is just a potpourri of a book not aimed at any specific group of readers in particular. In fact, the reader should read on only if the questions raised in this chapter have troubled the reader at some point in time or the other.

While this chapter raises questions, Chapter 2 briefly discusses the assumption of rationality in decision-making among human beings. Chapter 3 familiarizes the reader with the problem of simple prisoner's dilemma and takes a look at some of our traits in the backdrop of the dilemma. Chapter 4 deals with iterative prisoner's dilemma, with examples drawn from our everyday observations as well as some constructed parallels. Chapter 5 underscores how it helps to cooperate even if one were selfish in the extreme sense of the word. Chapter 6 deals with issues of self-regulation and fairness, and looks into how self-regulating and fair we are as a people vis-à-vis those elsewhere. Chapter 7 takes a look at the free-riding phenomenon and our own propensity to free ride. Chapter 8 deals with how and why we are a country that can neither impose systemic solutions to any of our problems nor stick by these solutions. Chapter 9 answers the poser contained in the Prologue. And finally, for those who may be more spiritually inclined, Chapter 10 links game theory with some of the teachings of the Gita and explains the role of dharma in a game theoretic context. On to rationality in the next chapter.

CHAPTER 2

On Intelligence and Rationality

Your city is reeling under a severe heat wave, and the water tables have disappeared to the depths. The local government has made impassioned pleas to its citizens to shower only every alternate day for a month, by which time the worst of the crisis will be over. You have had a hot night after a power cut and would love nothing more than a nice cold shower first thing in the morning. But today is your turn to skip bath. Your overhead tank is full and a shower will surely rejuvenate you. Forgoing it could benefit the city, but only marginally. Is it rational to sacrifice your shower? Is it rational to inconvenience yourself when it will barely make a difference to the city as a whole?

PEOPLE ARE RATIONAL

In the preface I mentioned that my interest in game theory and social dilemmas drew me towards behavioural economics.

Let me explain game theory and behavioural economics a little more. The Oxford English Dictionary defines game theory as 'the mathematical analysis of competitive strategies where choices depend on the action of others, e.g. in war, economics, games of skill, etc.' According to Wikipedia, it is 'a hybrid branch of applied mathematics and economics that studies strategic situations where players choose different actions in an attempt to maximize their returns'. Game theory was first developed as a tool for understanding economic behaviour and then by the Rand Corporation to define nuclear strategies. Since then, it has travelled just about everywhere: in academic fields as diverse as biology, psychology, sociology and philosophy. It has been applied to animal behaviour and to political science. That is why game theory is also accepted as the theory of social situations. In fact, Thomas C. Schelling and Robert J. Aumann won the Noble prize in economics in 2005 for their work in game theory applied to arms race, price wars and actual warfare. Thus game theory is not something arcane and academic but a very practical tool for understanding day-to-day social situations. And for me, our Indianness—exemplified by, say, why we routinely jump queues—provides a rich and fertile ground for applying this theory if only to help us introspect on whether we genuinely approve many of our own actions in the social context.

Behavioural economics (and behavioural finance, both are closely related) applies research on human and social perceptions, frailties and biases for insight into economic decisions—the role of reason in the economic choices we make. As you can judge, psychology too comes into play. Here is an example. Let us say that both you and I have a flight to catch at 8 p.m., though our destinations cities are different. Let us say we decide to share a cab and perchance get caught in a traffic jam of the kind that happens once a decade. We are stuck for several hours and as we cannot turn back we end up reaching the airport anyway, albeit four hours late. Pure economics will tell us that if our losses or other consequences such as having to stay an extra night, pay for the cancellation of the tickets, etc. are all identical, our regret at missing the flights will also be more or less identical. But now, suppose the airline staff tells me, 'Sorry sir, your flight left on time,' while you are told, 'Oh how very unfortunate sir, your flight was three hours and fifty-five minutes late and they just closed the aircraft's doors!', who feels more sorry about missing the flight? Here lurks psychology mixed with economics for you, which often explains everyday situations much better than pure economics alone can.

A number of game theorists have contributed to the body knowledge of modern game theory. John von Neumann and Oskar Morgenstern were among the early theorists who dealt essentially with non-cooperative games with 'pure rivalries', that is, zero-sum situations, where one can win only at the cost of another. However, it was Nobel laureate John Nash who first turned his attention to rivalries with mutual gain, that is, non-zero-sum situations, where one does not have to win at the cost of another, as both parties can emerge winners. Following his works, albeit through the *Scientific American* articles of Hofstadter, has helped me understand our characteristics like rationality, irrationality, egotism, selfishness, antagonism, competition, collaboration and cooperation as Indians vis-à-vis peoples elsewhere in the world. All versions of game theory essentially assume extreme rationality of human beings—rationality consistent with extreme selfishness. However, the theories also prove both theoretically and empirically that such selfishness need not come in the way of cooperation, and hence in the overall betterment of the human race.

At the same time, the works of Daniel Kahneman, Amos Tversky, Richard Thaler and many others in the past twenty-five years or so have challenged some of the core assumptions of the rationality of people as economic or calculative beings. Much of their work is in the context of finance theory.

Why do people behave as they do? With respect to economic behaviour, finance theory does have some answers. Human beings are supposed to be rational in decision-making with regard to their economic choices. Among the assumptions of rationality in economics are that the risk level remaining the same, people expect higher returns; expected return remaining the same, they seek lesser risk; for every incremental unit of risk, they seek at least the same level of return as they sought for the previous unit of risk, and so forth. Economic theory dubs those who act in accordance with these assumptions as 'rational' or 'utility maximizers'. A little reflection reveals that these are not unreasonable assumptions and most people can be termed as rational beings in matters of economic choices.

What is utility maximization? Normally a child likes sweets and dislikes bitter things, such as medicines. But you may be able to persuade a child to swallow a bitter pill provided you also ply the child with some candies. The more pills you want a child to swallow, the more candies you may have to offer as inducement. If you had to offer two candies to persuade the child to swallow the first bitter pill, it is unlikely that the child will accept anything less than two candies, and probably will want more, for the second bitter bill and so forth. In short, the child will accept a combination of pills and candies in proportions that would satisfy him best. In more technical language, the child is maximizing his utility and hence acting rationally. In the world of investments, returns and risks are to an investor what candies and pills are to a child. That lemming-like investors may well be utility maximizers, and hence rational, was reinforced when certain laboratory experiments found rats to be utility maximizers in the sense assumed by finance theory. See Appendix 1 for details.

In this respect, game theory is no different. As a theory of social situations, it also assumes that people are rational and coldly calculating. In other words, people are assumed to behave in their own selfish interest. Even an altruist is assumed to do a 'selfless' deed only for the happiness and satisfaction he derives from such an action. Hence, he is also assumed to be acting in his own self-interest. Typically, in social dilemmas, one has a choice between doing what is best for oneself and what is best for the group to which one belongs. For example, whether to chuck our kitchen trash at the neighbourhood crossing or walk the extra block to the municipal dump is a dilemma most of us living in this country are familiar with. All of us know that walking that extra block to the municipal dump is the right thing to do in the interest of the society as a whole. Yet, personally, it seems such a waste of time, considering that the streets are anyway dirty and the kitchen trash of just one more household is unlikely to make much of a difference to the overall sanitation of the city. Why sacrifice one's self-interest for the sake of the community when one can throw away the trash without any fear of retribution? Selfishness seems to tell each and every Indian that it is entirely rational for us to chuck our trash all around. This results in the huge garbage heap of a country of over one billion people. Clearly, rationality needs a relook.

OF COURSE WE ARE INTELLIGENT AND RATIONAL

Rational thinking and intelligence go hand in hand. As the human being is more intelligent than other animals, he is also more rational. As far as intelligence goes, Indians are perhaps second to none in the world. This view, though subjective, is based on several observations.

For example, I often see how a kid barely into his teens in the neighbourhood vegetable shop does rapid-fire mental maths, so that before you have put half a kilo of this and three-fourth kilo of that, and two and a half kilos of yet another vegetable in the bag, he spits out the final amount you have to pay. Or how a waiter in a dhaba can take orders orally from half a dozen customers simultaneously, with each one ordering three or more dishes, and rarely make a mistake while serving the orders from memory. Or how a roadside mechanic can solve complex mechanical problems with ingeniously improvised tools and solutions. Or how two schoolboys in Bangalore can launch a hand-made rocket.

On the other hand, elsewhere in the world, I have seen sales assistants swiping ten lemons ten times through the auto-coder instead of multiplying the price of one by ten. I have seen a dry-cleaner refusing to accept a shawl for cleaning because the price list available did not include a shawl. Of course one could blame this on the systems-driven society that the Western world is, which gives the individual relatively little scope for deviation from norms except when that individual is systemically empowered to make deviations. But somehow I cannot imagine an Indian shop assistant not using his head to price a non-standard product under similar circumstances. In India nearly every situation is encountered as a first-time situation and people respond to them as such—so for sheer survival one has to be extremely intelligent. You have to be extremely intelligent to grasp in a split second that the traffic cop has no vehicle to chase you with, and so you can jump the red light with impunity. Or judge in the flash of an eye whether he has a pen and notebook with him to jot down your number—if he does not have these with him, you assume it is safe to ignore his signal to you to pull over. Or to figure out, when on impulse you spit copiously on the street from the safety of your balcony and a poor pedestrian happens to intercept your wad, that there is precious little he can do, short of DNA testing to prove that it was you who spat.

We cannot shrug off the fact that we use much of our intelligence to figure out ways of circumventing every law, regulation and norm in a bid to do better for ourselves, and to twist and turn every available opportunity and prospect to our immediate advantage. For example, a cooperative society of an apartment block may be contemplating upgrading or repairing its lifts. The society asks all the residents to pay a certain sum to do this. It does not take long for the quick-witted ground-floor occupants to realize, and quite rationally, that as they do not need to use the lift it is not in their interest to pay towards its upkeep. Tenants on the upper floors realize, equally rationally, that it is not worth their while to pay for the upkeep of the front garden, the benefit of which is largely reaped by those on the ground floor. Likewise, the non-swimmer or the non-gym-user sees little reason to pay for the maintenance of these common facilities. The end result is that we have an apartment block with a defective lift and badly maintained front, a decrepit swimming pool and non-functioning gym. The quality of life of the community and the real estate value of the building take a nose-dive.

As individuals, we seem more rational and intelligent than those in Western societies. Yet, it appears that the sum total of our individual utilities do not maximize our collective utility as a people.

It is such contradictions in our understanding of the rationality of the socio-economic man that behavioural economists like Kahneman, Tversky, Thaler and others have tried to explain, based on some deep insights into how most people take decisions. They have shown that in a surprising number of situations people were not rational in the sense postulated by economic theory. When it came to receiving benefits they behaved one way; when it came to giving away benefits they behaved differently. When probabilities of risks and rewards were high they behaved one way, and quite the reverse when those probabilities were low. People often found it rational to free ride, yet not always and certainly not everyone. When questions were posed one way, they responded one way, and when the same questions were put differently, they responded another way, and so forth.

For example, two samples of doctors are drawn from the same population. One sample of doctors are presented the following poser:

The bird flu epidemic is expected to hit your town and it is estimated that 600 people will die. Which of the following two drugs, A or B, will you recommend to combat the epidemic, given the following information?

If Drug A is used: 200 will be saved
If Drug B is used: 1/3 chance that all 600 will be saved, and 2/3 chance that nobody will be saved.

It seems a greater percentage of the respondents vote for Drug A.

Now the second sample of doctors from the same population, who are not exposed to the above poser, are presented a different looking poser:

The bird flu epidemic is expected to hit your town and it is estimated that 600 people will die. Which of the following two drugs, C or D, will you recommend to combat the epidemic, given the following information?

If Drug C is used: 400 will die

If Drug D is used: 1/3 chance that nobody will die, and 2/3 chance that 600 will die

It seems a greater percentage of the respondents vote for Drug D.

A moment's reflection however reveals that the two posers are in fact identical and that Drug A is the same as C and B is the same as D, except that in the first case the problem was presented in the form of life and in the second case in the form of death. And yet, even among professionals, the choice was different depending on how the problem was posed.

So exactly how rational are we as world citizens? How exactly do we define rationality in the social context? Is there a meta-level rationality? What is it anyway? How does our rationality impact our decisions? How does our meta-level rationality impact our decisions? Can selfishness lead to cooperation? These questions are at the back of many of the situations that we shall encounter in the subsequent chapters, even as we search for the aperture that may give us a better insight into ourselves.

CHAPTER 3

Simple Prisoner's Dilemma and We the Squealers!

A city boy, Ram, moved to the countryside and bought a goat from an old farmer for Rs 1000. The farmer agreed to deliver the goat the next day. But the next morning the farmer went to Ram and said, 'Sorry son, but I have some bad news. The goat died last night.'

Ram replied, 'Well then, just give me back my money.'

The farmer said, 'Can't do that. I have spent it already.'

Ram said, 'OK then, just unload the goat.'

The farmer asked, 'What are you going to do with a dead goat?'

Ram: 'I'm going to raffle him off.'

Farmer: 'You can't raffle off a dead goat!'

Ram: 'Sure I can. Watch me. I just won't tell anybody he's dead.'

A month later the farmer met Ram and asked,

'What did you do with that dead goat?'

Ram: 'I raffled him off. I sold 500 tickets at Rs 10 apiece and made a profit of Rs 3990, net of the Rs 1000 I paid you.'

Farmer: 'Didn't anyone complain?'

Ram: 'Just the guy who won. So I gave him back his Rs 10.'

Ram grew up and eventually became a successful Indian Businessman.

THE SIMPLE ONE-TIME DILEMMA

Prisoner's dilemma, first identified by Melvin Dresher and Merill Flood of Rand Corporation in 1950 and subsequently articulated by Albert Tucker in its current form, has come to occupy a prominent place in game theory. The problem statement goes like this: Assume you and I are conspirators in a crime. Both of us are supremely selfish and coldly rational. We are being interrogated in two separate cells and are not allowed to communicate with each other. The interrogator tells you that he has enough circumstantial evidence on each of us to put both away in the slammer for two years each. However, if you squeal on me and help him prosecute me, he will let you off right away but give me five years behind bars. He also tells you that he is making an identical offer to me (though you and I cannot communicate). You reflect upon the offer momentarily and ask, 'But what if both of us confess everything?' 'Sorry,' says he, 'in that case I will have to put you both away for four years.'

The payoff matrix for the above problem is shown in Figure 3.1. The years behind the slammer are indicated as negative numbers since it represents the undesirable consequence.

		You	
		Do Not Squeal	Squeal
I	Do Not Squeal	(−2, −2)	(−5, 0)
	Squeal	(0, −5)	(−4, −4)

Figure 3.1   The Prisoner's Dilemma Payoff Matrix

Being supremely selfish and coldly rational, our response to the offer is guided in terms of what is in our best self-interest. Emotions such as friendship, decency, fairness and graciousness are irrelevant. Jesus's unsettling query 'Does it profit a man to gain the world if he loses his soul?' does not disturb us. Our only concern is to get as little time as possible in the slammer.

Now, here is our dilemma: Should we squeal against the other? As rational and intelligent beings each of us would argue thus: 'If he decides to squeal, it is best that I squeal too. Why should the scoundrel romp home free while I get the slammer for five years? On the other hand, if he, the fool, is naive enough not to squeal, it is in my interest to squeal and romp home free while he enjoys his stay behind the bars.' So no matter what I do, your 'rational' choice is to squeal. So you squeal.

I, on my part, cannot trump that logic either and so I follow suit and squeal. The squeal–squeal decision earns both of us four years in the slammer. But if we had decided not to squeal, we would have served only two years. It is obvious that in order 'not to squeal' one need not be driven by higher-order values like friendship, kindness or altruism. 'Do not squeal', in fact, turns out to be the superior option even if we are supremely selfish and rational, though hardly a convincing one when you are one of the prisoners in dilemma.

HOW DO I GET YOUR GOAT?

Let us see if we can unwrap the dilemma a little more. Let us say that you have a yard full of bleating goats, but are short of liquidity, and I have money aplenty, but not enough goat meat. Providence puts us in touch with each other and we come to a one-time agreement under which next Monday, 9 a.m. sharp, you will tie a robust goat for me at a place of my choice and exactly at the same time I will leave a cheque for Rs 1000 at a place of your choice. Come Monday morning, you will go and collect my cheque and I will go get your goat. Our arrangement and circumstances are such that we will never ever come face to face with each other or even communicate with each other, once our one-time contract is concluded. We are both supremely selfish and act only in our best self-interest. Ethics, fair play, moral suasion and even legalities, all are assumed irrelevant.

Now if we both cooperate so that it results in a successful swap of goat and cash, let us say, we derive two units of satisfaction each; if I cooperate by leaving a cheque for Rs 1000, while you defect, leaving no goat at all, or leaving a sick goat or a lame goat or a goat that's all bones, you will derive four units of satisfaction, for it is fun to get something for nothing, while I derive a satisfaction of −1 as it stings to be duped; likewise if you cooperate by leaving a healthy and meaty goat and I defect by leaving a cheque that bounces, I derive four units of satisfaction for having got your goat for nothing and you derive −1 satisfaction; and, finally, if we both defect, we gain zero satisfaction point each. The payoff matrix for this arrangement is shown in Figure 3.2.

		You	
		Cooperate (C)	Defect (D)
I	Cooperate (C)	(2, 2)	(−1, 4)
	Defect (D)	(4, −1)	(0, 0)

Figure 3.2 The Payoff Matrix for a Prisoner's-Dilemma-Like Trade Agreement

You will find that the payoffs in Figure 3.2 are nothing but number 4 added to each payoff shown in Figure 3.1. For example −2, −2 in Figure 3.1 become 2, 2 in Figure 3.2; 0, −5 become 4, −1, and so on.

The payoff of 2 in Figure 3.2 is what Hofstadter calls the reward (R) for mutual cooperation; 4 the temptation (T) for non-cooperation; 0 the punishment (P) for mutual defection; and −1 the sucker's payoff (S). The reward, temptation, punishment and sucker's payoff in Fig. 3.1 are respectively −2, 0, −4 and −5. It is important to note that for a payoff matrix to represent prisoner's dilemma, two conditions must hold:

1) $T > R > P > S$
2) $(T+S)/2 < R$

The first condition merely ensures that no matter what I do, it is better for you to defect. The second condition ensures that if our agreement is of a more permanent nature, say, exchanging a goat for Rs 1000 every month, even if you and I lock into an arrangement where one month I defect (amassing 4 temptation points) and you cooperate (with sucker's payoff of −1 point) and the next month I cooperate (with −1 point) and you defect (with 4 points), neither of us will do better. In fact we shall do worse (only 1.5 points a month on average), than if we were both cooperating every month (earning 2 points every month).

As we set to operate our one-time agreement, my mind begins to mimic the familiar prisoner's dilemma argument. If you are sucker enough to cooperate and leave a healthy goat—ribbon and all—for my benefit, it is in my rational self-interest to defect on my obligation and leave you a bad cheque, and earn 4 temptation points. On the other hand, should you be vile enough to defect and leave a sick goat or no goat at all, I am still better off defecting, that is, leaving a bad cheque. At least, we will be even with no one earning any points. No matter what you do, it is in my best interest to defect; so I will defect!

The only problem is that you are as smart as I am and think exactly the same way as I do (don't most of us Indians think the same way?). Consequently, we both defect and are left without something of value that we wanted. We are both left with punishment points. Had we both cooperated, keeping to our respective ends of the bargain, we would both have reaped a reward of 2 points each.

PRISONER'S DILEMMA AND OUR EXPORTERS

The goat trade just described is a common occurrence in India. For instance, a small exporter in India manages to bag a one-time export order based on a promising sample sent by him earlier. Let us say the payment is to be received by cheque, or in the form of a simultaneous import of some other product. The conditions are very close to the simple prisoner's dilemma situation. The two parties have an agreement—each party has to deliver something that the other party desires, in accordance with an agreed timeframe and specifications. The two parties probably will not meet face to face, as they are oceans apart. Nor are they likely to engage fruitfully in expensive legal battles if either party defaults on its obligation. What are the odds that either the Indian or the foreign trader will default on his obligation? I would wager more heavily on our Indian exporter defaulting, say, by supplying spurious consignment that falls drastically short of the agreed standards or weight and so on. We are not talking of cheats and fraudsters here. A perfectly normal, well-respected Indian businessman, acting rationally, believes that he is amassing more temptation points and his shrewd mind grasps the situation as a simple one-time prisoner's dilemma situation, under which it is very clear to him that no matter what the other one does it is better for him to defect.

I was amused to read in the press (February 2005) about the UK–India imbroglio over the former banning red chilli powder import from India, amidst allegations of large-scale adulteration by Indian exporters. Only a week before this sad controversy erupted, I was told by a friend that when he was posted in South Korea with a multinational bank, in the 1970s, he was witness to an export outrage by India. Apparently, after striking a deal to import red chillies from India, the Koreans found the very first consignment adulterated with red-brick powder. The Koreans emptied the entire consignment in the high seas, vowing never to source red chilli powder from India. Things have not changed much with our business practices, have they?

This is not a one-off case. A news item titled 'Early birds tip the apple cart' in the *Economic Times* (5 July 2005) said that apples from India's largest producer, Himachal Pradesh, would not be at their scrumptious best that year because the producers, in a hurry to make a fast buck, had plucked them much before the harvest month and treated them chemically to get the red glow. The haste had adversely affected the export of apples.

PRISONER'S DILEMMA AND JOINT VENTURES

A similar non-cooperative behaviour indicative of misplaced understanding of self-interest is often seen in our joint ventures. For instance, a typical Indian businessman will go any length to ensure that he takes a 51 per cent stake for himself, or his company, to ensure he is the boss who calls the shots in the joint venture. Shortly afterwards, when the foreign partner talks of expanding the business, and there is need for more capital, he is irritated that he has no money to bring into the venture. He thinks it so unfair that the foreign partner should bring all that money and then expect him to match it. They wish to overtake his 51 per cent stake, he reasons. He is unable to see why these overseas partners should wish to derive as much benefit from the joint venture as himself. Could it be that they entered the joint venture for the same reason as he did, namely to make as much money as possible? He lives in a state of constant anxiety wondering whether the partner is benefiting more from the partnership than he is, his earnest attempts to prevent that notwithstanding. Or else, what is the partner doing continuing in the joint venture with a 49 per cent stake?

He now brings his razor-sharp mind to bear on the problem, namely, how best to bend, twist and rattle the terms of the joint venture agreement so as to outsmart and outwit the partner. The poor overseas partner will soon discover that in our Kafka-like judicial system, he cannot enforce the joint venture agreement in any case. In short, our businessman smartly defects, while the partner is trying to cooperate. (I am sure you notice that I am stretching the point somewhat, just to make a point. After all there are the Enrons of the world out there too, who would make our hero look like a retarded five-year-old.)

Soon the overseas partner wishes to get out of the venture. In the meanwhile the Indian businessman manages to get that one-time big payoff by buying out his stake for a song.

But that one-time payoff comes at the cost of a series of moderate payoffs that would have been possible through the partner's technical support, greater financial strength, overseas market support and so on, had the Indian businessman continued to cooperate.

ARE WE SO SMART AFTER ALL?

Let us go back to the apple exporters. Let us say had they 'cooperated', that is, waited full season before plucking the fruit, they would have earned a net profit of Rs 2 a kilo. On the other hand, by 'defecting' or plucking the fruit before the harvest season and ripening them artificially, they could earn a profit as high as Rs 5 a kilo.

Can our rational producers, who are presumably not one-time traders, maximize their 'satisfaction points' with their defecting behaviour? They may earn Rs 5 a kilo (temptation points) but only at the cost of an ensured income stream of Rs 2 a kilo (reward points) that they would have earned in the future through cooperation. Thus they fail to maximize their long-term rewards for an immediate temptation. What makes it so difficult for us to realize that the temptation points we earn owing to immediate temptation comes at the cost of a string of future rewards?

For some peculiar reason, we are happy with that one-time skimming of temptation points and lack the ambition to amass those strings of rewards.

PRIVATELY SMART AND PUBLICLY DUMB

When I jump a queue or a red light, or throw that garbage on the sidewalk, I am taking a rational 'squeal' decision, since it seems to get me ahead of others or make life easier for me. Here I am being privately smart. But then, as others are no less rational, intelligent and smart, they too start squealing for the same reasons and, before we know it, we have unruly traffic, filthy streets and stinking urinals. So collectively we are all worse off, just as the two prisoners in the dilemma. And then we complain about a dirty country, a polluted city and appalling traffic. In short, publicly we emerge dumb.

Or when a corporate firm puts up ghastly giant-sized billboards all over the city with little regard for aesthetics, or pollutes the environment or makes low-cost, inferior goods to score over competition, and the competitor, with identical logic, puts up ghastlier billboards, pumps more effluents into the river or cuts more costs to produce shoddier products, it is being privately smart. But before long, we have an ugly, polluted country full of shoddy products. And then we raise concern about corporate governance! Clearly, we are publicly dumb.

Consider this. In many countries, one often sees buildings where every balcony, every balustrade and every window maintains, over centuries, the original plan, colour and appearance. Such aesthetics ensures that the real-estate value of that property does not drop. Of course the enforcement of regulation in such matters in these countries is very stringent, shaping the behaviour of the buildings' occupants. But in a democratic society, regulations are made by 'us'; so who is to blame if stringent regulations are not in place, as in our country? And how can we enforce such regulations given our resolute resistance to any attempt at such enforcement? If three of us put up a building together, one of us will cover our balcony with glass windows, the other will put out an awning and the third will close his balcony with a concrete wall to extend his room size. In short, we 'squeal'. And if such conduct violates any city regulation at all, aren't the enforcers of the regulations 'squealers' themselves when they turn a blind eye to such violations for ulterior considerations? At yet the next higher ply, aren't the politicians who 'transfer' the inconvenient enforcers (the upright and strict enforcers) being 'squealers' too?

Which ply is initiating the cascading effect of squealing all around? We? The regulators? The politicians? We are all part of the '*we*', the *meta We*. We are forever squealing—squealing against each other . . . squealing in our organizations . . . squealing against the system . . . squealing against our towns, our cities, our nation . . .

OUR FATALISM

We also squeal when we do not champion issues, leaving it to others to take the initiative. The others, in turn, do exactly the same, that is, leave it to someone else. So we are left with a thousand issues facing the country and no champions in sight.

'What difference can I alone make?' is our well-reasoned attitude. What does it matter if I alone do not vote? Will the country's corruption rating on Transparency International get any better if I stop greasing a palm? Surely the country's traffic problems can't get any worse just because I slip through that red light? What does it matter if I alone come in late for the meeting? Surely the entire pool can't get dirty just because I urinate in it? How can my not throwing that piece of paper on the street clean up the whole city? What does it matter if I alone keep my high beam on while driving at night? Will the country's water table get any higher just because I alone invest in a rainwater-harvesting system for my house or remember not to run my wash-basin tap full blast while shaving? This is how we usually reason. This fatalism, ingrained as it is in our psyche, is visible in our day-to-day actions. To give an instance, I was once waiting for my bags at an airport carousel. The baggage of a particular flight had not arrived even an hour after the flight had landed. The airline officials too were missing. While most passengers had begun to get fidgety, one of them took it upon himself to look for the duty manager. There were at least four or five in the crowd who advised that lone gentleman not to waste his time, saying, 'It will make no difference, take it easy.' And as soon as the much-delayed bags arrived, the passengers departed hastily with their baggage, not wishing to spend any more time and energy complaining.

From the prisoner's dilemma viewpoint, the catch here is obvious: if an attitude is rational for me, it is rational enough for everyone else. Such an attitude invariably leads to the squeal–squeal situation, where everybody is left worse off.

The opposite phenomenon—'But everybody else is doing it'—is equally common, and leads to the same behaviour. Everybody is being corrupt, so why shouldn't I accept that bribe? Everybody is throwing garbage on the street, why shouldn't I? Everybody is jumping the queue, why shouldn't I? . . . Here again we are squealing.

These dual attitudes reflect the extent of our fatalism, our mute acceptance of circumstances, our unwillingness to believe in ourselves and the complete subjugation of the self. I was once travelling in rural Bihar in a Jeep. It took me some time to figure out that the pedestrians who stooped down to their waist and the cyclists who dismounted and adopted a likewise posture as the vehicle passed them were in fact conditioned to paying their respect to the authority that a Jeep—the standard vehicle of local officialdom—represented. There was total resignation to their fates writ large upon their faces. They were not about to challenge their low status in society. Their fatalism was complete.

Things are not very different in cities either. Again and again I have noticed so-called VVIPs nonchalantly jumping queues and going ahead of hundreds of passengers at airports. Such is our awe of authority that I rarely see passengers challenging these worthies or even joining those odd ones who do challenge such interlopers.

Our behaviour is not unlike that of the herd of enormous bison we get to see on National Geographic, watching in mute resignation a couple of lionesses kill and eat one of their own. How often do we read of scores of people standing mute witness to a rape in a suburban train? Nobody else is trying to take on the rogue, so why should I or how can I alone do it, we reason. What is happening is not because of me, so why should I intervene?

And yet, one in ten times, inexplicably those bison on National Geographic are shown to turn on the lionesses. And when they do, the victim simply stands up and walks off. In other words, if only we believed in ourselves and did not hide behind what others are doing or not doing, it is always easy to retrieve the situation. But we seldom do so. So fatalistic have we become that we no longer even seem to suffer a guilty conscience when we give or take bribes, when we stand mute witness to gross injustice or when we allow our rights to be trampled upon by the powerful and the mighty. In the language of prisoner's dilemma, each one of us defects in such situations, and as a consequence our fatalism becomes a self-fulfilling prophecy.

The same 'what can I alone do' syndrome is perhaps also the reason we do not always espouse larger causes; it is also perhaps the cause for our low achievement levels; and reason too for our placid acceptance of the filth, corruption and chaos all around us.

PRISONER'S DILEMMA AND THE BIG PICTURE
Though seemingly an abstract problem, prisoner's dilemma encompasses our lives more pervasively than we imagine. For example, both India and Pakistan argue exactly as the two prisoners cited in the prisoner's dilemma, and arrive at the 'rational and well-reasoned' decision to go nuclear—a squeal– squeal behaviour that results in the two countries forgoing the

opportunity to save millions of rupees that could have been used for better health, poverty alleviation or primary education, not to speak of reduced risk of mutual annihilation. In fact, much of international politics takes the same route, whether it is in the context of negotiations on world trade, climate change or banning of whaling operations.

TOO INTELLIGENT FOR OUR OWN GOOD?

At times perhaps we are far too intelligent for our own good. We use our intelligence to quickly see through the fact that no matter what the other does it is 'better' for us to squeal. So we make sure we squeal like impaled pigs every time a choice to squeal or not to squeal presents itself.

Of course this is not to deny that the prisoner's dilemma has a universal applicability and Indians are no exception in being prey to the dilemma. But what is striking is that, in most situations, we Indians do not even see any dilemma. Defection seems to be our default setting. The exasperating thing about prisoner's dilemma, particularly in a country like ours, is that even after all these discussions, if the same problem is posed all over again, it is given that we will defect all over again. Because you know that if I know that you are not going to squeal on me, I would surely squeal on you (and vice versa), as I am supremely selfish, and my squealing guarantees me freedom at your cost. So you figure that you must squeal on me. That makes a pair of us thinking exactly alike, which invariably leads to a squeal–squeal situation.

Recognizing that there is indeed a dilemma would be the first step towards resolving the dilemma and achieving cooperative behaviour. But it appears that we are nowhere near that realization. The problem gets more complex as we encounter iterative and many-people prisoner's dilemma type of situations.

Let us explore the iterative prisoner's dilemma situation in the next chapter.

CHAPTER 4

Iterative Prisoner's Dilemma and the Gentleman Strategy

A reporter once asked a farmer to divulge the secret behind his corn, which won the state agricultural contest year after year. The farmer confessed it was all because he shared his seed with his neighbours. 'Why do you share your seed when you'll be competing with them in the contest every year?' asked the reporter.

'Why sir,' said the farmer, 'don't you know? The wind picks up pollen from the ripening corn and swirls it from field to field. If my neighbours grew inferior corn, cross-pollination would steadily degrade the quality of my corn. If I am to grow good corn, I must help my neighbours do the same.'

THE ITERATIVE PD

Real life is seldom like a simple one-time prisoner's dilemma (PD) situation or a one-time interaction between two parties.

More often than not, it comes closer to what may be called an iterative, repeated or ongoing PD situation. We interact with the same party over and over again. While any one interaction may be akin to a one-time PD situation as described in Chapter 3, a series of such interactions with the same party over and over again results in iterative or repeated PD situation—more like exchanging a goat for a cheque every month.

To take the goat-trade from Chapter 3 a little further: Let us assume that you and I get into a lifelong (rather than a one-time) arrangement to leave a goat and a cheque for Rs 1000 respectively at mutually agreed spots, on the first of every month at 9 a.m. Again, the exchange arrangement is so impersonal that we will never meet face to face or even communicate with each other, and we are both supremely selfish. Our payoff matrix remains the same as before, namely as represented in Figure 3.2.

How will our arrangement progress? I will soon start wondering how early in the arrangement it will be best for me to defect with my payment, even as you are harbouring similar thoughts regarding your goat, tempted by those alluring four points—double the normal reward of two. Both of us would be careful not to start the transaction with a defection. In the first month, I will cooperate (C) and so will you, and our first exchange, which is a C–C type, will help us pocket two points each. But our temptation to defect is very real and soon we will start sweating out our strategy to earn the temptation points.

The questions that arise here are: What shape will this ongoing trade eventually take? When will it be best for either party to defect on the arrangement to maximize one's temptation points? Given that the first one to renege on the agreement gets to keep four points while the naive cooperator gets a −1, isn't the first defector better off? So why should one continue to cooperate, given that we are supremely selfish?

SUPREMELY SELFISH

What is it to be supremely selfish? Let us assume that for a number of years both of us continue with our C–C transactions as it becomes obvious to us that we are better off cooperating, amassing two points every time. Or is it so obvious? Assume that just when you are dozing off, collecting those boringly slow two points every month, a little bird brings you the good news that I am a nonagenarian, on dialysis thrice a week, with one kidney removed and the other failing, lying in the intensive cardiovascular care unit (ICCU) of a heart hospital, just having undergone a quadruple bypass surgery, with a hip fracture that I suffered when I slipped in the bathroom when I had that heart stroke, all compounded by some infection I picked up in the ICCU. Surely you do not expect me to survive the month. Are you not tempted to defect now? After all you may well get away with your last defection, gathering four points without suffering any adverse consequence of retaliatory defection from me. In fact the surer you are that this is my last month to live the more tempted you are to defect. I too would be, if the situation were reversed. This is what we mean by being supremely selfish and that is the assumption underlying total rationality. Since amassing more points for oneself is the sole necessity here, sentiments such as friendship, loyalty, compassion, fairness and goodwill are of little relevance and so we defect.

LET'S GET REAL

The fact is that we don't trade only goats. We trade many other things—both tangible and intangible. We also have trading relationships with more than one party—in fact with many parties. Again, not all our exchanges are trades. They may also be non-commercial, such as exchange of greetings. We call these social interactions. Even these interactions are trade-like in the sense that we derive satisfaction points from them too, which are not unlike the satisfaction points we derive from trade interactions. For example, when you greet a neighbour and he responds to your greeting affably, you have a C–C like behaviour and you derive some level of satisfaction. But when your greeting elicits no reciprocal greeting you have a C–D like behaviour and you derive negative satisfaction from the interaction. In other words, real life is not just a repeated PD-like situation between two parties: it involves repeated interactions among hundreds or even thousands of people.

MAXIMIZING POINTS

There are millions of us scampering around in the system, interacting with each other off and on, like particles in Brownian motion dashing against each other individually, jointly or severally. Now if we scamper about long enough, sooner or later each one of us in the system ends up interacting with all the others. Assume we are able to recall the nature of our last interaction with a party—whether it was a C–C type,

D–D type or C–D type interaction—so that we can strategically decide what to do in response this time. Remember once again that each individual is supremely selfish and is only trying to maximize his total points over the multiple interactions over time.

Let us also assume that I am not an ailing nonagenarian, but a young and hearty individual like you, which means the chance of either of us coming down with a life-threatening ailment that could motivate the other to defect soon is bleak. And in this cauldron of Brownian motion, you are interacting with not just me but many others like me. How soon would either of us be tempted to defect in order to collect four temptation points from each of our transactions, thus maximizing the overall number of our points? And what is the best strategy to maximize our points?

THE BEST STRATEGY

Reverting to our monthly goat-trade agreement, let us assume that after three months of C–C type of transactions I get a mite impatient with this boring state of affairs, where I never seem to get the better of you. So on the first of the fourth month I decide to defect (while you cooperate), giving rise to a D–C transaction that gets me the coveted four points, while you lose one point.

As I would be ahead of you by five points (I got ten points in all: two, two, two and four, while you have five points: two, two, two and minus one), what should be your best strategy to maximize your points in due course? Suppose you take the 'Never Again' or 'Massive Retaliation' stance, according to which 'I will never ever be the first one to defect, but if you defect once, I'll never play ball with a scoundrel like you ever again.' Then we are both doomed to earning no more points off each other, since all future transactions between us are doomed to be D–D type.

If I had had the good sense to contain my impatience instead of rushing to defect, both of us could have enjoyed the benefits of a prolonged mutual cooperation, thus enhancing my collection of points. But now, my defection and your retaliation with Never Again strategy will cost both of us all future satisfaction points.

Now, suppose my defection had not been deliberate but due to an unavoidable circumstance, and on the first of the fifth month I leave a cheque as usual but find no goat in return as you have decided 'Never again'. It soon becomes clear to me that there will be no more goats from you to me and all our transactions are doomed to be D–D type.

However, suppose you did not take my one-time defection so much to heart and went looking for my cheque the fifth month and found it, though you leave no goat in return as I had defected the previous month. You realize I am not an all-out scoundrel. Not seeing your goat at the delivery site, I too would understand that you wish to get even with me for my last month's defection. After this hiccup, from the sixth month, life could well be back on a smooth sail, with each of us back to earning our two points a month.

So is Massive Retaliation the best strategy? No, as it impairs all further accumulation of points. So what other strategy could you have adopted, given my fourth-month defection? Perhaps you could have allowed me one chance, that is, one more defection, before your massive retaliation. This would have earned both of us the future string of two points from the fifth month onwards, had the reason for my defection in the fourth month not been deliberate. If I had defected deliberately, I might get your goat yet again, leaving no cheque, thus exploiting your goodness and earning four points once more; but neither of us would earn anything from each other any more.

Yet other possible strategies for you could be to allow two more defections to me before retaliating, or springing some random defections of your own, such as, say, one, two or three random defections every ten interactions, and so on. Of course my own defections or when or how to retaliate against your defections would be part of my strategy.

Clearly, our objective of maximizing satisfaction points appears to be best achieved through a long string of rewards of twos that we can garner from mutual cooperation, rather than through temptation points of four gained by defecting.

So asking 'What's the best strategy?' is the same as asking 'Which of the strategies will ensure maximum points for me from the sum total of my transactions with others over a prolonged period of time?' There does not appear to be a single answer. For example, my simple strategy could be to take you to the cleaners if I know that your strategy is to give at least two chances before retaliating. If there are enough suckers giving two chances apiece, I could make a living amassing four points twice off each godly man. After all we have a billion-strong population and I could get seriously rich exploiting the naive. On the other hand, if I knew the population is made of massive retaliators galore, I would go easy on my propensity to defect.

AXELROD'S EXPERIMENT AND THE GENTLEMAN STRATEGY

In the late 1970s, Robert Axelrod, the mathematician and political scientist best known for his work on the evolution of cooperation, investigated if there was any one strategy that outperformed the others.[1]

The experiment, structured as a competition, invited experts in game theory to send in algorithms which could maximize the total points in the iterative PD environment in the Brownian motion scenario, as delineated earlier. The experiment required each program to outline how it would respond to a Cooperate or Defect (C or D) move from another competitor, with the payoff defined as in Figure 3.2. The objective of the algorithm was to maximize the total number of points accumulated for itself over a large number of transactions. Here is a summary of the experiment.[2]

There were fourteen entries that qualified for the competition, with program lengths ranging from seventy-seven lines to a mere three words. Each program was effectively trying to compete with all the other programs by first 'understanding' the other's behaviour before unleashing its specific strategy on the other. So here was each program trying to find chinks in the other's armour, thrusting into those chinks or parrying; now enticing the other to continue cooperating while itself defecting to wrest those four temptation points; and now trying to guess what the next move of the other was going to be, so as to decide whether or not it was worth defecting; here trying to appear like a perfect gentleman who almost always cooperates except to defect once in a while to gain those four seductive points after a long series of twos; and there trying to exploit the 'simpletons' who were found to be naive enough to give two or more chances to the defector before retaliating, and so forth.

Axelrod made each strategy interact with every other strategy 200 times, and the tournament itself was run five times to smoothen out random statistical fluctuations in the outcomes, so that nobody could accuse his results of suffering from statistical vagaries.

At the end of this marathon competition, the program that won the tournament was the shortest of the many entries, comprising essentially three words—Tit for Tat—entered by the famous game theorist Alfred Rappaport. The Tit for Tat strategy was truly simple—'Never be the first to defect; thereafter do what the other one did the last time.'

The Tit for Tat strategy always 'plays' a C to begin with. The response of the other party, say also a C, resulting in a C–C transaction, is stored in memory. The next time the same party is encountered, Tit for Tat plays a C again (remember, it never defects first) and so on, until it encounters a D against its C, resulting in a C–D transaction and stores that fact in memory. The next time it encounters the same party, it plays a D. But the strategy holds no permanent grudge. If the other party responds with a C this time, resulting in a D–C interaction, it plays a C the next time. On the other hand, if the other plays a D once again, Tit for Tat returns a D. At any future time, should the other party revert to C, in the move after that Tit for Tat returns a C, and so on. In short, Tit for Tat bears no long-time grudge. But it does seem to subscribe to that old adage 'You cheat me once, shame on you; you cheat me twice, shame on me.'

TIT FOR TAT NEVER WINS

The Tit for Tat strategy never amasses more points than any one strategy at any point in time. In other words, it never ever wins against any other strategy. At best, it equals the score vis-à-vis another individual. This is because, by never defecting first, it is always the first to suffer a deficit of five points, by losing a point and giving away four points to a defector consequent to a C–D transaction. And when it defects in turn in the next move, it remains at a disadvantage if the other strategy continues to defect and all future transactions between the two degenerate to D–D type. On the other hand, if in the next move the other strategy reverts to cooperation while Tit for Tat defects in retaliation, it merely manages to equal the score by recouping the deficit of five.

Then how did Tit for Tat come out with top honours in Axelrod's experiment? How is Tit for Tat a winning strategy if it never wins against any one strategy?

This is where we need to understand the overall objective of the tournament more deeply. The objective was to accumulate as many points as possible for oneself, taking all the interactions into account, and not to win against any one strategy or individual, or even score maximum number of wins against any, leave alone all, individuals.

THE GENTLEMAN STRATEGY

It does not take long to realize that Tit for Tat is a gentleman strategy. It never defects first. But it does get provoked to retaliate. It does not believe in 'turning the other cheek'. Gentleman, yes; Gautam Buddha, no! A defecting individual is rebuked with a defection next time. So a defector soon learns that, unless he undoes the damage caused by his earlier defection, he cannot expect to profit any further from his interactions with Tit for Tat. Finally, it is also forgetting and forgiving. It holds no long-time grudge like the Never Again strategy. It has a memory only for the other's last action and all earlier memory is erased, since the earlier defections, if any, have already been 'paid for' by the retaliatory defections in the following moves. Lastly, it is not envious of others doing well, so long as it does well enough for itself. With all such attributes, one cannot but see that Tit for Tat is simple and truly a gentleman strategy.

To be nice and simple, to get provoked in the face of injustice, to forget and forgive and not be envious, all are gentlemanly traits. People with such traits do make more friends and go further ahead of others. Perhaps that answers why the Tit for Tat strategy came out on top.

A WINNING STRATEGY

Once you begin interacting with the Tit for Tat strategy, you soon see through its simplicity. You realize that you can always bank upon it not to defect first. You realize too that if you defect, for whatever reason, it will defect the next time and not cooperate until you correct the imbalance created by your defection. You learn that, if you wish to profit from Tit for Tat, it pays not to defect with it very early in the interactions. Suppose you are an occasional defaulter, where you cooperate most of the time but defect occasionally, say 10 per cent of the times. If you defect against a Tit for Tat, the consequence is that you are either up or, at worst, equal in score to Tit for Tat in due course. If you compensate for your defection by cooperating in the move after Tit for Tat punishes you, and go back to cooperation, you can hope to earn a lot of reward points of twos in the future together with Tit for Tat. But what if you run into a Never Again strategy? Clearly, you will never ever be able to earn any profit points from it after your first defection. This will not be the case if Tit for Tat and Never Again interact, since neither of them ever defects first and hence will earn a perennial stream of two points from each other, amassing a large number of points. But Never Again loses out to Tit for Tat because, when it comes up against the occasional defaulter, it stops all future interactions in a fit of massive retaliation. On the other hand when Tit for Tat comes up against a default from an occasional defaulter, it retaliates in the next move, but reverts to cooperation once the defaulter does the same, thus earning a profitable string of twos in the future.

So even though Tit for Tat may not win against any one single strategy, it manages to amass more points than most other strategies in the long run.

AGAIN AND AGAIN!

Axelrod did not stop there. He carried his experiment a good deal further using computer simulation. He ran a similar but larger tournament, where the competitors were provided with detailed results of the first tournament along with an explanation of the strategic qualities of niceness, simplicity, provocability and forgiveness that had made Tit for Tat the best strategy in the first tournament, so that experts could try and work on more sophisticated strategies that could outperform Tit for Tat. The new format of the tournament put the competing strategies through a variety of situations to ensure that a strategy was truly and genuinely robust and not a flash in the pan.

What happened in the subsequent tournament is remarkable again. Rappaport returned his original strategy, Tit for Tat, in its original form. Others turned in strategies like Tit for Two Tats. There were also some 'villainous strategies' that tried to amass points by preying upon the tolerance of the 'good strategies' like Tit for Two Tats. Then there were strategies that would almost never defect first, but use a random number generator to defect once in a while, say 1, 2, 5 or 10 per cent of the times, hoping their defection would go unpunished. In all, this tournament attracted sixty-six entries.

Taking a cue from biological evolution—survival of the fittest, which results in a greater number of progeny in the next generation for the successful species—Axelrod picked the best strategies from each simulation run, and increased the weightage of such strategies in the subsequent run of simulations. What does this imply? If a certain strategy happens to be robust, it may be reasonably assumed that the strategy will multiply itself faster in due course, as more and more people come to adopt it. Axelrod simulated this realistic scene by ensuring that the best strategies in one run of the tournament were made more numerous in the next generation of the tournament. By varying the proportions of the best strategies in the next generation, Axelrod was able to arbitrarily create a large number of environments in which various strategies competed with each other.

As the experiment took off, in the initial runs, it was found that many villainous strategies were ranked very high—in fact among the 'best', alongside the likes of Tit for Tat—in terms of amassing maximum number of points as they prospered by preying upon strategies such as Tit for Two Tats. As the experiments progressed to subsequent generations of simulations, with the proportion of the best strategies (which included the villainous ones) increasing in each successive generation of runs, it was found that in due course the villainous strategies started dropping out of the race.

The reasons, though a trifle perplexing, are not too difficult to fathom. To begin with, as the villainous strategies gained ground in the environment, the good strategies started thinning out. As the 'exploitable' good strategies began disappearing, the villains had less and less simpletons to exploit and consequently they too began to thin out. As successive runs of the tournament progressed, it turned out that strategies like Tit for Tat that were not exploitable and other similar strategies began to gain ground.

Not only did Tit for Tat emerge with top honours, its rate of growth in the successive generations was also among the highest. Yet, predictably, Tit for Tat never beat a single one of its competing programs!

TIT FOR TAT IN EVERYDAY LIFE

So what if the Tit for Tat strategy emerged numero uno in the iterative prisoner's dilemma tournament? How does it relate to our daily lives? Let us take a simple situation. I spot a colleague walking towards me at some distance in the office corridor. While there is no law that requires us to greet each other, it is the polite thing to do. So I greet him but he, for some reason, looks through me. A 'royal ignore' is how I read it. In my mind, I 'cooperated' while he 'defected', so we have here a C–D like transaction.

The next time I encounter the same colleague, I have to decide whether or not to greet him. If I were a massive retaliator, I would ignore him forever. Alternatively, I could adopt the Tit for Tat strategy. Or else, I could follow the random strategy or 'two chances' strategy or any other strategy.

As colleagues we are socially called upon to decide whether or not to greet each other every time; hence we are in a sort of iterative PD situation. What if I had adopted the Never Again strategy? I would have ignored the colleague completely, no matter whether or not he greeted me again. Chances are after one or two such encounters he would stop greeting me. As a result, neither of us would ever be of much collegial comfort to each other.

On the other hand, if I were to adopt the Tit for Tat strategy, I would try to find a reason for my colleague's action. As the light was behind me, he could not see my silhouette very clearly in the dark corridor. Or maybe he was preoccupied with some problem and wasn't really looking at me carefully. Or he thought I was waving to somebody behind him and moments later he probably reflected on the possibility that I had after all waved to him, but before he could reciprocate my greeting, I had already turned the corner. So the next time we meet, I remain uneffusive while he, knowing his earlier omission, makes amends with a hearty greeting. I am now satisfied that he had not really ignored me the last time. The next time we pass each other again, we greet heartily and this continues.

If my colleague had deliberately ignored me the first time, he would have continued being stand-offish when we met next and I could have reciprocated with my own cold treatment (Tit for Tat), leading to a D–D behaviour forever.

You can see how Tit for Tat scores over Never Again, even though 'morally' both are similar in that they never defect first.

Never Again makes a strong value judgement on a fellow's actions based on a single experience. On the other hand, Tit for Tat is more tolerant of human frailties and allows room for one-off defections and always allows a defector to recover. Never Again is judgemental, while Tit for Tat is practical.

TIT FOR TAT IN POLITICAL LIFE

I have always been intrigued by the rather regrettable success of Tit for Tat in politics. It is common to see two politicians belonging to different parties go for each other's throats. Yet, come elections, the two get together, like long-lost siblings in the final reel of a Bollywood flick, to form a coalition. Unfortunately, and mostly for all the wrong reasons, politicians understand the power of Tit for Tat far too well and never ever hold long grudges.

Let us explore in the next chapter whether competition can lead to cooperation. Before that, you may want to take a look at Appendix 2, which presents a digression on pseudo dilemmas.

CHAPTER 5

Can Competition Lead to Cooperation?

Sometimes cooperation emerges where it is least expected. During the First World War, the Western Front witnessed horrible battles. But between these battles, and even during them at other places along the 500-mile line in France and Belgium, the enemy soldiers often exercised considerable restraint. A British staff officer on a tour of the trenches remarked that he was:

> . . . astonished to observe German soldiers walking about within rifle range behind their own line. Our men appeared to take no notice. I privately made up my mind to do away with that sort of thing when we took over; such things should not be allowed. These people evidently did not know there was a war on. Both sides apparently believed in the policy of 'live and let live.'[1]

LIVE AND LET LIVE

Tit for Tat won Axelrod's tournament not by beating other players but by eliciting behaviour from them that enabled them as well as Tit for Tat itself to do well. It was so successful in eliciting mutually rewarding behaviour (a la 'live and let live') that it amassed the highest overall number of points. In short, these experiments showed that when interacting with many different players, in non-zero-sum situations of the kind we have been discussing, one does not have to do better than others to do well for oneself. Letting others do as well as or even better than oneself is fine, as long as one is doing well enough for oneself. That is what is being gentlemanly all about. Consider this in the context of the comments we hear about how we Indians often compete not by performing better than others but by pulling others down.

CRABS IN THE BUCKET

We often equate ourselves with crabs in a bucket from where no crab would escape since any crab trying to get out of the bucket is sure to be pulled down by the others inside. This syndrome is nothing but a reflection of our dissatisfaction with others doing better than ourselves. So if we cannot do as well as them, we are perfectly happy if they will do as badly as us. Since it is easier to pull someone down than to pull oneself up, we usually choose the former. In effect, we want parity with our neighbour or our competitor, no matter how. In effect, in an iterative PD situation, we do not play the gentleman strategy. We play crabs in the bucket. Consider these recent examples of our policy making.

Foreign Direct Investment

Let us take our foreign direct investment policy. Just as the investment begins to come in as a consequence of a liberal policy, we begin to have some misgivings. There must be some unfathomable reason for those foreign investors to come flocking in. Could it be that, unwittingly, we have made the environment too good for them? Surely, if the environment is so good for them, it must be bad for us? With these thoughts nagging us, we soon announce a change in the policy. We would probably make some feeble gains, with a brownie point here and a political point there, resulting in a one-time payoff, but the decision would cost us enormously in terms of international credibility and sustainable future benefits.

Higher Institutions of Excellence

Or consider this. Few would seriously dispute that the Indian Institutes of Management (particularly Ahmedabad, Bangalore and Kolkata) are among the few Indian institutions of higher education that have done exceedingly well over the decades. They have built up international reputations. They have shown the ability to create potentially large corpuses. They have ensured that no deserving student has to forgo education in these institutions for lack of financial resources. They have done this by charging relatively high fees from those who can afford and subsidizing those who cannot. They have shown their ability to be free from government funding. Perhaps it would have been best for the government to allow these excellent institutions to continue their good work within a well-defined mandate, and expend its supervision and resources over institutions and areas that are crying out for reforms. Instead, what have some of the recent governments been doing? Working overtime to curtail these institutions from building reasonable-sized corpuses, preventing them from going global, denying them autonomy to decide on their fee structures, inhibiting them from bringing in foreign students or forcing their directors to seek permission of the human resources and development ministry for travelling abroad. If the rest of the government institutions cannot measure up to the standards of a few like the IIMs, they can always be brought on a par by pulling these centres of excellence down a few pegs.

Entry of Foreign Universities

The proposed bill to regulate foreign universities in India is yet another example. The bill ostensibly requires foreign universities coming to India to provide 49.5 per cent reservation (15 per cent for scheduled castes, 7.5 per cent for scheduled tribes and 27 per cent for other backward castes), not indulge in 'profit-making' and instead follow the fee structure suggested by the University Grants Commission. At the risk of oversimplifying, it would appear that, since our universities are unable to match the standards of the universities abroad, we are quite happy pulling them down to our level. At a time when we should be questioning reservations based on considerations other than merit, we are busy foisting the irrational, homegrown reservation policy not merely upon domestic institutions but also on foreign universities to bring about a lowest common denominator. While we ought to be looking at rationalizing our domestic fee structures for higher education, we are busy dragging the others down. Why would the foreign universities come to India on these terms, considering our very own IIM Ahmedabad pulled out of opening a Mumbai campus rather than acquiesce to the state government's demand for a reservation policy for Maharashtrians? How can we ask for the participation of foreign universities when they have nothing in it for them? Where is the 'live and let live' policy here? Clearly, we are more worried about what they might get out of coming to India than what we might get out of it.

Rational Fools

Amartya Sen calls those taking such decisions, including the likes of our exporters, joint venture partners, et al., 'rational fools'.[2] It would appear that as a country we often act like the biggest 'rational fools' of them all. And why not? After all those who make the various structures, systems and units of the country are just ordinary fools like you and me.

IPD and TVS

We do have happier examples as well. This is a story retold by Suresh Krishna, chairman of Sundram Fasteners Limited of the TVS Group. His father, T.S. Krishna, the doyen of the TVS Group, narrated this story to him in the early 1960s.

In the mid-1940s' economy, diesel engines were in extreme short supply in the country. Any trader who so much as held an import licence for a diesel engine could command a hefty premium on its import price in the domestic market. Most of the local traders in the then Madras Presidency did not miss out on this golden opportunity to realize that premium, and were able to realize Rs 4000 to Rs 5000 on a diesel engine as against its import price of Rs 1100. T.S. Krishna, however, continued to sell the engines at the standard mark-up of around 25 per cent. The local business community thought him naive, if not downright daft, for forgoing the opportunity to maximize what we would call today his 'shareholder value' (SHV). Having narrated this story, T.S. Krishna asked his son, 'Son, of all those "SHV maximizing" [terminology in quotes mine] traders, do you recall even one? But the TVS Group remains a name to reckon with. Our customers remain loyal to us.'

The SHV maximizing businessmen who squeezed the war-torn economy for all it was worth by extortionist pricing showed non-cooperative behaviour (D behaviour) vis-à-vis their customers. While they amassed large one-time points by turning the pockets of their customers inside out, the customers in due course (remember the iterative PD) shifted their loyalties elsewhere, denying the former continuing points to be earned through mutual cooperation. That probably explains why those smart businessmen of the 1940s faded away without a name. T.S. Krishna, on the other hand, by continuing the normal pricing during the shortage period, had exhibited a basic cooperative behaviour (C behaviour), thus winning their loyalty and continued mutual cooperation.

In short, T.S. Krishna was a gentleman in the PD framework, who never defected first, giving little cause for his clients, shareholders and other stakeholders to defect either, and thus amassed a long string of reward points both in economic and in non-economic terms. Had Krishna argued, 'Well everybody is doing it,' like most of us argue, he too would have sold his engines at a higher mark-up and the TVS Group may not have been what it is today.

Clearly, on account of such cooperative behaviour, groups such as TVS and Tatas from the old economies and Infosys among the new ones have managed to retain the loyalties of their customers and shareholders over the years and it is this behaviour that probably shapes corporate governance or business ethics. Probably, Krishna had never heard of such terms as corporate governance and social responsibility, but he did what a simple and decent man would do. And this made good business sense in the best traditions of iterative prisoner's dilemma.

The Name-Change Companies

There were any number of companies in the 1990s that indulged in all kinds of 'defection' acts while making their public issues. They came to be known as 'name change' companies. Their defections ranged from opacity in sharing information with the investing public to deliberately misleading them, from gross overpricing of the issues to inserting an 'infotech' or just 'tech' into their names, and so on. These companies made their one-time big payoffs in temptation points, at the expense of the cooperating investors who were naive enough to invest in such companies. But these companies have hardly had the credibility to come back to the investing public for more capital, as the investors retaliated with their own 'defection' on such companies by starving them of any further capital. If these companies intended to be in existence for the long haul, well, they ceased to, thanks to their defective behaviour. But as scamsters out to fleece the naive over a one-time PD game, they did earn their temptation points. Unfortunately our weak legal system and poor enforcement machinery make it easy for one-time PD players to succeed.

WE HAVE HOPE YET

In all, being nice, simple, provokable, forgiving and unenvious—virtues learned from Tit for Tat—does help to go a long way. What Axelrod showed is that in an iterative PD situation, even if one is supremely selfish and sees nothing beyond maximizing satisfaction points for oneself, it pays to be nice, simple, provokable, forgiving, unenvious and the one who never defects first. We do not have to be cooperative, following values like ethics, fairness and integrity. Pure self-interest, as in the case of intense competition, will do nicely.

Another feature of prisoner's dilemma is that it can never be resolved if you approach the problem from outside, that is, from the other's viewpoint first. The problem offers a resolution only if you approach the problem from inside, that is, from your own self. As long as you begin your argument saying, 'Whatever the other does, it is better for me to defect,' you can never resolve the dilemma. The only way to resolve the dilemma is to ask, 'What's the right course of action that could be best for us both?' In this sense, the resolution to PD is inward-looking and not outward-looking. If you look inwards, no matter how selfish you are, you will find the correct resolution to the dilemma. Needless to say, what holds true for you also holds true for the other. If both of you look inwards to arrive at the correct answer to the dilemma, you do arrive at it.

So it seems cooperation can emerge out of selfishness; it can emerge out of competition. At first glance, manipulative and exploitative behaviour might appear to get us ahead, but in the final analysis, being simple, nice, forgiving and self-righteously provokable gets us much further.

CHAPTER 6

Self-regulation, Fairness and Us

First they came for the Jews
and I did not speak out
because I was not a Jew.
Then they came for the Communists
and I did not speak out
because I was not a Communist.
Then they came for the trade unionists
and I did not speak out
because I was not a trade unionist.
Then they came for me
and there was no one left
to speak out for me.

—Rev. Martin Niemöller (1937)

PUBLIC HYGIENE AND US

What do you think is the biggest challenge confronting the country? Exploding population? Abject poverty? Pathetic basic education? Woeful primary health care? Scarcity of clean drinking water? Unhealthy pollution levels? Near absence of a justice delivery system? Runaway corruption? Pathetic infrastructure? Dangerously high criminalization of the polity? Depending on whom you ask, it could even be too high or too low real interest rates. Thank God, Veerappan is no longer a national problem. More visible and insidious than any of the above are our stinking toilets, which reflect not just the quality of our public hygiene and collective aesthetics but also our attitude towards sanitation. What makes us this way?

As nationals of the world's largest democracy, we would like India to have a permanent seat on the Security Council of the United Nations. We would like India to be taken seriously by the world as a country of one billion. We would like foreign direct investors to throng in. We want India to be a major international tourist (including what we call health-tourism) and information technology destination. Yet, we see no inconsistency of these aspirations vis-à-vis keeping the country carpeted with garbage and filth. What is more, we see no irony in our posturing before the world as a representative of a morally superior culture. We see no ignominy in accepting the state of our towns and cities, perennially tottering on the verge of epidemics. Our tolerance towards using the streets as toilets goes to show that we see little shame in accepting that people can live without basic dignity.

In fact, at a national level, we do not even recognize our public hygiene habits or disorderliness as a problem. We read of the Singapore President, S.R. Nathan, exhorting his people to keep their toilets clean, as if they were not already in the cleanest country in the world. Clean toilets were also the concern of a renowned management thinker, Frederick Herzberg, of the Herzberg's Hygiene Factor fame. In India, nobody, either before or after Mahatma Gandhi, seems to have thought it seriously worthwhile to address the issue of our national sanitation.

Forget the dismal state of our public urinals, even the national carrier is occasionally known to suffer from toilet bowls brimming over mid-flight. Clearly, this has nothing to do with our poverty, or lack of resources or the economic status of the users. It is our defect–defect behaviour and utter lack of self-regulation at work.

We find examples of such behaviour wherever we look. Every day we see people sweeping the dust and garbage from their homes and shops on to the streets. We see entire housing colonies, hospitals and vegetable markets dumping their garbage into the next street. We see municipalities dumping their garbage on the outskirts of their cities. The garbage shoving goes on. Finally, what we are left with is not a garbage disposal system but a garbage redistribution system. As a consequence we must walk with our heads hanging down— not merely for the shameful condition of our streets, but also for fear of stepping into some inevitable muck. It is possible that you have done your bit and fought against filth, squalour and corruption. But it is equally probable that in time you have come to adopt an attitude a parent has towards an unruly child—you may be exasperated, or you may not be terribly proud of the child, but thanks to the parental bond, you cannot love the child any less.

MATCHING SENSE OF PUBLIC AESTHETICS

Our collective aesthetics is another case in point. Ghastly hoardings on ugly scaffoldings; untidy signboards on shops, roadsides and boundary walls; narrow, unplanned and perennially dug-up and potholed roads; dusty, unpaved roadsides full of squatters; roadside temples; free-roaming fauna; criss-crossing telephone and electric wires; unkempt shopping complexes; buildings with unmatched balconies and awnings, where no collective norms can ever be enforced; grubby trains and buses; undisciplined traffic . . .

Parallel roads and covered drainages, it would seem, went out of fashion with Mohanjo-Daro and Harappa civilizations. Today, we just erect buildings haphazardly and hope that in due course we will be able to carve out a road through the mess. We dump construction material on the sidewalks and even roads in the comfortable knowledge that either the authorities will not pull us up or that their ever-ready palms can always be greased. We release our sewage into our seas, rivers, lakes, streams and canals with impunity. We carve out ghastly sores on our hills and mountains in the name of mining rocks and earth. We let loose three-wheeled rattlers all around us, causing noise and air pollution. We smell human faeces and see bubonic rats on the tracks and curse the railway authorities, but never think of not using the toilets on the stationary train or not throwing that food waste on the tracks. Undoubtedly, our defect–defect behaviour lies at the root of our filth, corruption and chaos.

LACK OF SELF-REGULATION

Why is our sense of public hygiene and aesthetics so abysmal? In all the cases just mentioned, lack of self-regulation plays as much a part as lack of regulation. Unfortunately, self-regulation does not appear to be our strong suit.

For example, take our traffic. Why is it always in a shambles? The reasons are several. To begin with, we are a nation that regards traffic signals with contempt and will not voluntarily obey the signals until we are forced to. To make matters worse, we have very few traffic signals. Most smaller roads, even in big cities, often have no traffic lights. And, more often than not, the signals do not function properly, thus eroding public respect for them even further. As a consequence a red signal is hardly a cue to stop or a zebra crossing hardly a reminder to slow down for the pedestrian.

Even if there is an attempt at enforcing traffic rules, we disregard it except when the enforcement process is very physical. Ever noticed how, during peak hours, the Mumbai police use rope cordons to hold pedestrians at bay before the traffic lights clear? Or on occasion how constables have to stand in front of the lead vehicle to keep the entire rank of vehicles behind it at bay, till traffic from the other direction clears? Have you observed how frequently we do not stop our vehicles for even a minute to allow an ageing pedestrian or a child to cross the road? Left to ourselves, we are inconsiderate and uncaring.

Weak self-regulation and weaker regulation

It does not take an 'intelligent Indian' long to figure out that in the wee hours there is little vehicular traffic and no traffic cop in sight. So what purpose is to be served by his stopping at the red light? Whom is he trying to prove his traffic sense to anyway? In short, he will jump the red light when there is nobody to stop him. Soon this trait emboldens him into jumping red lights not only during late hours, but at any time there is no cop in sight. It is again only an incremental step for him to jump the red light even when a cop is in sight, if the latter has no vehicle to give chase. Even if the traffic cop has a vehicle at his disposal to chase him, what will the consequence be, after all? A hundred-rupee fine? Not a serious enough deterrent. Even that may be easily mitigated with two curled-up twenty-rupee notes deftly thrust into the eager palms of the constable. So he is now jumping red lights in broad daylight under the very nose of a traffic cop. Not only does the 'intelligent Indian' defy all rules and norms, he also graduates to honking at you should you be conscientious enough to stop at a red light when he wishes to jump. In his calculation, it is a waste of time to stop at red lights, particularly if there is no risk of being stopped by a constable, and it saves him a few precious minutes. With little patience or self-control, before long we too begin to mimic the 'intelligent Indian' and soon we have on our hands a traffic nightmare. A mass-scale defect–defect behaviour.

Why does the system not penalize traffic defectors? Why does it not confiscate their driving licence? Why don't we have a system that will encourage a traffic cop to book traffic offenders? How is it that such systems work everywhere in the world except in our country? This being the case, should we be surprised if our already weak propensity to self-regulate grows weaker?

Ithaca, Ahmedabad, Bangalore and Elsewhere

Richard Thaler cites the example of a one-lane bridge across a creek behind Cornell University in Ithaca.[1] During traffic hours, there are always many cars on either end, waiting to cross the bridge. In a wonderful display of self-regulation, four or five cars will cross the creek and then the next car in that direction will stop to let four or five cars from the other direction to cross and so on. One realizes this will hardly work in New York, leave alone in Indian cities and towns.

There is another standard practice in many countries that is testimony to the self-regulation of the residents there. On most railway crossings, there is only a thin bar that comes down when a train is about to cross, which spans half the road (on the side where the traffic is supposed to move). Similarly, there is another half bar on the other side of the crossing, so that technically all you have to do when the bars are down is zigzag through the two bars to get across the rail lines. But I have never seen anyone do that. Everybody waits patiently on his side for the bar to lift, before he moves on.

In contrast, there are two trademark practices I have seen in Ahmedabad. These practices are more or less rampant in other Indian cities as well. Ahmedabad is dotted with railway crossings. The railway gates there, like those anywhere else in the country, are formidable affairs. These gates invariably span the entire width of the road, and then some, on either side, with a skirt-like barricade hanging all the way to the ground. But this barricade means as much to the gritty pedestrians and two-wheelers as the closed drawbridges of forts meant to the determined Vikings. Most of these dedicated souls can be seen lifting the iron skirt and squeezing themselves and their vehicles through.

Trademark practice number two: Whenever the railway gate is down at any crossing in Ahmedabad, as vehicles begin to queue up on the left side of the road, others begin to queue up on the right-hand side of the road, hoping to be the first to get through to the other side as the gate lifts. Needless to say, those on the other side of the barrier have the same idea, so that when the railway gate lifts what we have is a most frustrating bedlam, as citizens try to outdo each other on a logjam, compounded by honking, pushing, shoving, cursing, scratching and denting. This happens in every Indian city. People never realize the futility of their action. Nor do the traffic police realize that they ought to penalize the stalwarts who line up on the wrong side of the road. Clearly, we lack self-regulation just as much as we lack regulation.

Now imagine if we were all lined up on the left side of the road, as expected of us. Let us say there is one defector who decides that it pays to line up on the right-hand side of the road so that as the gate lifts, or the light turns green, he can zoom ahead of the others. For some reason, instead of discouraging such a defector, most often than not, we all end up aping him.

Yet another defect behaviour is to take off from a crossing when the digital clock on the red signal shows five or six seconds to go. If thousands of commuters have internalized this habit, we have a disaster waiting to happen. Sure enough I witnessed one such accident in Bangalore, where two vehicles coming from perpendicular directions in those last few seconds rammed into each other. As in most other cities of India, self-regulation is an alien concept for commuters in Bangalore.

In contrast, peoples of other nations appear to have a greater sense of self-regulation. Even in the Philippines, Malaysia and Thailand, nations comparable to us in many ways, I have observed much better traffic compliance. In Beijing, I have seen the taxi driver stop at every red signal even at 2 a.m., though there was no other vehicular traffic at that hour and no traffic constable in sight. Of course any comparison with China evokes a discussion on democracy and other forms of governance, as if democracy must be blamed for all our failures and the relative lack of it in China credited for all their successes.

Going back to Thaler, he also writes of the delightful rural areas around Ithaca, where farmers leave their fresh produce on a table by the roadside, along with a cash box strapped to the table. The rates are displayed on the table and the customers simply pick up the veggies they want and drop the money into the thin slit opening in the box. The farmers in Ithaca apparently have the right amount of faith in their fellow citizens. They know that enough citizens will pay for the corn, yet they also know that, if the cash box is left unchained, somebody might simply walk away with it! A similar system is followed in Europe for newspapers.

Can this system work in our country, where even the slot machines are manned? If you think such a system is impossible in India because the poor may be tempted to cheat, think again. The economically well-off too cannot be trusted even when it comes to coffee. Let me cite an example.

At a leading business school I suggested an Ithaca-farmer-like system for dispensing coffee and tea for its faculty, staff and students. Back-of-envelope calculations showed that, even if half the tea or coffee guzzlers did not pay, the system would break even, given the relatively high cost of employing four to five men to serve coffee morning and evening and to pick up empty mugs strewn all around. The suggestion was turned down without any deliberation in the faculty council. Some of the questions raised were: How can we create a trust-based system in a formal organization, knowing fully well that some people will free ride on the system? Why should others pay for these free riders (even though the others were not paying any higher, mind you)? Why should we subsidize free riders?

Here is another example. In the 1980s the annual fee in leading business schools in the country was equivalent to the price of a good pair of shoes. Or two maybe. And the monthly cost of living in the hostel for a student was probably about the same. But the socialistic thinking of the day obliged the public-sector banks to provide educational loans to needy students at interest rates as low as 4 per cent, when the market interest rates were 12 per cent and more. What is more, the banks were not prone to chasing their bad loans assiduously, given the relaxed accounting and regulatory environment of those days. As a consequence, full repayment of the loans by the students after they passed out was more an exception than a rule. The result: most of these loans turned bad on the books of the banks, and in due course they stopped giving educational loans. Most of these students had the best jobs the country had to offer and many of them had fabulously paying jobs abroad. The loans outstanding against them, in most cases, would at best have equalled a dinner for six at a five-star hotel. Surely, these defectors were not economically challenged, at least not when it was repayment time?

FAIRNESS, TRUST, SELF-REGULATION AND US
Over the years, I have posed the following question to MBA students in Europe (representing several nationalities) as well in India: 'If you were dining in a restaurant in a new city that you are certain never to visit again, will you tip the waiter who served you?' (The question was originally posed by Hofstadter.)

Clearly, this is a one-time PD situation, at least from the individual's perspective. I have observed that the proportion of students from the Indian subcontinent responding in the negative is typically higher than the European students.

The same phenomenon appears true when you shift the focus from customers to vendors. For example, one might say that a vendor on a railway platform has less reason to be courteous to a passenger or serve him quality food, considering the passenger is not likely to patronize him again. An Indian vendor is far quicker to grasp this fact than his counterpart in the West. I recall witnessing a one-time PD situation on a train a couple of decades ago. A teenaged boy on the platform was selling cold water in terracotta cups to the passengers on the train, at twenty-five paise a cup. The train was about to chug off. Here was this gentleman in the compartment with a twenty-five-paise coin clutched between his thumb and forefinger, insisting that the boy hand over the cup of water first, before he let go the coin. And the boy was afraid to let go the cup without having the coin in his grasp, lest the man not release his grip on the coin before the train pulled away. It was several seconds before the tussle was resolved. To me this has remained a representative example of our distorted sense of self-interest and our mistrust of others. Of course this is not to say one hasn't had some wonderful experiences as well, where complete strangers spontaneously come up to help in a variety of situations.

I think there is a lot of wisdom in the old adage that urges one to treat others as one would like to be treated oneself, that is, fairly. That wisdom merely requires one never to be the first to defect.

But whether that adage is followed in compliance or rejection, cooperation or defection, as a rule or as an exception must depend on whether or not the majority of the people are instinctively fair, cooperative and self-regulating. Interestingly, behavioural economists have done considerable work in the area of fairness as a constraint on profit seeking, though in a somewhat different context. (Their work essentially questions or modifies the assumption of rationality as assumed by standard finance theory.) Some discussion on the nature of work relating to self-regulation, fairness and trust will give the readers a better insight into what is typically regarded as non-cooperative or unfair behaviour and whether or not we punish the unfair.

What's Fair?

Let us consider a situation where there has been a truckers' strike and suddenly vegetables in the market have disappeared.

Before the strike, onions were retailing at Rs 20 a kilo. Now which of the two situations below is fair or acceptable?

A1. A vendor who has a large stock of onions from before ups the price to Rs 35 a kilo.
B1. A vendor who does not have any previous stock and is paying a much higher price for the onions, on account of the more expensive alternate transport arrangements, prices the onions at Rs 35 a kilo.

Most respondents faced with the above situations are bound to find the first scenario unfair, and the second fair, even though the buyers are called upon to pay the same price under both situations. Clearly, it is not the final action, but the motivation underlying the action, that decides what is or is not viewed as cooperative or fair behaviour.

Kahneman, Knetsch and Thaler present many such situations.[2] For example, which of the following two situations (the numbers here have been changed to suit Indian currency) is unfair?

A2. There is a shortage of a popular car model and the waiting line for delivery has grown to two months. A dealer has been selling this car at the list price. But now he prices the car Rs 25,000 above the list price.
B2. Another dealer has been selling this car at a discount of Rs 25,000 to the list price. Now he prices this car at the list price.

A majority of the respondents view the first dealer to be unfair, and the second one acceptable, even though both dealers call upon the buyers to pay Rs 25,000 more than before. In other words, the first scenario is likely to be viewed as a non-cooperative behaviour.

Here are some more situations.

A3. A landlord rents out a house. When the lease falls due for renewal, the landlord learns that the tenant has recently taken a job very close to the house and admitted his children in a school close by. Figuring that the tenant is unlikely to move away under these circumstances, the landlord raises the rent by 30 per cent.

B3. A landlord rents out a house. When the lease falls due for renewal, upon learning that similar houses in the neighbourhood are going at much higher rentals, the landlord raises the rent by 30 per cent.

The respondents typically find the first situation unfair, but the latter one quite acceptable. Any deliberate exploitation of the special circumstance of an individual is viewed as unfair or non-cooperative behaviour. (Recall the Chennai businessmen in the TVS story who exploited the special dependence of their clients during the post-war period.)

A4. An airline, during peak tourist season, finds that there are four tourists desperate for a last-minute ticket. The airline decides to auction the ticket on the spot to the highest bidder.

B4. An airline is trying to recruit a software expert at a time when there has been a big lay-off of professionals from the software industry. Four candidates, all equally qualified for the job, are shortlisted. The airline asks each candidate to quote the lowest salary he would be prepared to accept and then offers the job to the lowest bidder.

In both the cases the airline's conduct is regarded as unfair or non-cooperative by a majority of respondents, presumably because the airline is trying to profit from competition among its potential passengers or employees. However, the first situation becomes quite acceptable when respondents are told that the proceeds will go to a charitable cause.

Are We a Fair People?

I am struck by the differences in the response patterns to questions like the above between Indians and other nationalities. For example, consider the following poser of Kahneman et al.:

A5. How much will you tip for satisfactory service in a restaurant that you visit often, for a meal costing $10?

The mean response to the above question in their study was $1.28.

B5. How much will you tip for satisfactory service in a restaurant, for a meal costing $10, in a city that you are unlikely to visit again?

The mean response to the above question was $1.27.

The difference in tips between the two situations is not very much, indicating a high degree of self-regulation. When the same problem is posed before Indian respondents for a 500-rupee bill, I have often found the average amounts vary significantly in the two cases: around Rs 30 and Rs 5 respectively. Clearly, self-regulation among Indians is a weak trait. And it shows in every walk of life.

OUR RELUCTANCE TO PENALIZE UNFAIR CONDUCT IN OTHERS
Consider the following:

A6. There are two competing vegetable vendors near your house. One of them shuts down and as a consequence you notice that the other hikes his prices by about 5 per cent. In protest, would you switch your patronage to another vendor who may be ten minutes away from your residence?

While over two-thirds of respondents elsewhere in the world seem to say a more or less unambiguous 'yes' to the above question, I have observed that the Indian response is often less affirmative and qualified with various conditions, such as, 'It depends on the quality of vegetables', 'Depends on how inconvenient it is to go to the other vendor', and so on. Clearly, Indians invest a high degree of intellectual exercise in responding to such questions, but are far less prone to punish unfairness.

Here is a variation:

B6. A grocer close to your home runs a rather indifferent-looking outfit and keeps the frontage of the shop dirty and untidy, but on an average charges you 5 per cent less than another grocer about ten minutes away, whose shop as well as the frontage are immaculately clean (the products themselves are assumed to be equally clean in both outlets). Which of the two are you more likely to patronize?

And what if this situation is reversed, namely, the one closer to your home is the well-run grocer and the other is the untidy one? Will your choice flip? What if they are simply adjacent to each other?

While I have not polled these questions extensively, my experience and observation reveal that we Indians are less prone to take offence at the opportunistic vegetable vendor, as well as less inclined to pay for such intangibles as cleanliness. Our conduct may be economically rational in that we are not willing to pay the cost of an extra ten minutes of travel for penalizing the offending vendor, or that we are not willing to pay a premium of 5 per cent for rewarding the cleaner or the fairer grocer. But it seems that as a people we are less prone to pay an economic price to punish offenders or reward the good.

In Chapter 5 I argued that probably, as a people, we Indians are highly given to D–D behaviour. Yet, the illustrations A6 and B6 present a category of problems where we appear to exhibit a D–C behaviour! For example, in illustrations A6 and B6, when the other party (the vegetable vendor or the grocer) defects (by increasing the price opportunistically or running an untidy outfit), we end up cooperating by continuing to buy from that party. We do not seem to retaliate against the offending behaviour of the vegetable vendor or the grocer, for what we think is in our selfish interest.

At the same time, the illustrations A6 and B6 also seem to represent situations that appear to be win–win for the vegetable vendor (lower overhead costs) or the grocer, and us (lower purchase price). If so, that ought to represent a C–C behaviour. Yet, intuitively we can see that at a meta-level, the two behaviours are D–D in nature. How? The behaviour of a profiteering shopkeeper is inherently defective, because his exploitation of the customers cannot be to the customers' advantage. At the same time, the customers' inaction in not penalizing such a shopkeeper, which at first glance appears to cooperate with the shopkeeper, in effect amounts to a defection at a higher plane. How? Because by continuing to patronize such a shopkeeper, the customer reinforces the exploitative behaviour of the shopkeeper, leading towards a more exploitative group of shopkeepers in the society. And when shopkeepers in the society as a whole become more exploitative, everybody—including our customer who does not punish a defecting shopkeeper—suffers equally. Thus what appears to be a D–C behaviour between the shopkeeper and the customer at one plane is in fact a D–D behaviour when you bring the society into the picture at a higher plane.

We rue the fact that our laws rarely punish wrongdoers. True, the probability that a litterer, a traffic jumper, a thief, a ruffian, a hit-and-runner, a bribe taker or even a regular small-time crook will be caught and punished is rather low. But, in our personal lives, we are equally reluctant to enforce fairness. We would rather suffer unfairness, discrimination, corruption, unhygienic conditions, exploitation and such than strain ourselves challenging it.

How often do we take out a morcha or go on a hunger strike in protest against the appalling conditions of our roads, absence of clean drinking water, lack of sidewalks, zebra and overhead crossings, abysmal state of basic education, garbage on the streets, total breakdown in the justice delivery system, nightmarish traffic, corruption and such? But we do not hesitate to burn half a dozen buses or buildings (and a few people as well) for a finger wrongly raised in a cricket match. What exactly is our idea of unfair treatment?

ULTIMATUM GAMES

In a bid to inquire if capitalism is fair to the poor in an ethical, moral and material sense, behavioural economists such as Ariel Rubinstein and Ingolf Stahl have devised some delightful experiments and games to assess fairness or unfairness among people. You too can try them out at a party. Typically, games designed to measure fairness take the form of an ultimatum.

Consider this. You are given Rs 100. You are now asked to divide this amount between yourself and another person (whose identity is unknown to you) in any manner you wish. The other party may choose to either accept or reject your offer. In case the other party rejects your offer, neither of you receives anything (and that's the 'ultimatum'). Now that puts you in a pickle. Rationally, you would like to keep as much of the Rs 100 for yourself, say Rs 99 and offer Re 1 to the other. But you are aware that the other party may well reject the paltry offer. Your problem now is to figure out how much you should offer the other party so that the offer is not rejected and yet you retain as much of the Rs 100 as possible.

There are other variations to this game. You are told that you will be given Rs 100. You have to divide this amount between yourself and an unknown party. If the other party accepts your offer, the game will terminate. If that party rejects your offer, neither will get anything and the game will move to stage two. At this stage, the other party will be given Rs 25 (one may choose any other amount at this stage) and the roles will be reversed, but there will be no right of rejection in this final round.

Having received these instructions and Rs 100, how much will you offer the other party?

Conceptually the problem is simple, if you use the backward induction method. If the game moves to stage two, the other party can retain Rs 24 and offer you one rupee. Hence any offer higher than this in stage one should be acceptable to the other party. So you should offer Rs 25 in stage one.

If this second game is played often enough, especially by reversing the roles of the first and second parties, the participants begin to catch on that they need not share more than Rs 25. Yet, many still prefer to share a higher amount for reasons of fairness.

Published research indicates—and that's my experience as well when conducting these experiments outside India—that participants 'play it safe' and typically offer closer to 50 per cent in both stages of the game. But the percentage has been typically much lower in my ad hoc experiments among Indian respondents.

The idea of fairness has been pushed even further. In some experiments, the allocators are randomly given Rs 100 as dole or at the toss of a coin and asked to play the one-stage or the two-stage game. In another group the allocators are not chosen just by luck. They are made to 'win' Rs 100 by showing some prowess such as answering certain questions correctly and so on, in order to 'win' their right to be allocators, and then asked to play the same game. It is often found that those who 'win' their money the hard way tend to share a smaller fraction of their given bounty than those who just get lucky with their money.

Similar to the above situation is a variation involving two groups under two different scenarios. People are split into two different groups. In scenario one, a subject is asked to play the allocator against a receiver from his own group. In scenario two, a subject plays an allocator to a receiver from the other group. In such variations, allocators are found to be more generous to receivers from their own group compared to those from the other group. Apparently, the 'we–they' effect is quite pronounced in matters of fairness. People worldwide tend to be fairer to their own group (defined as they may be) as compared to 'others'.

In yet other variations, researchers have investigated whether allocators are fair even when their offers cannot be rejected, or how allocators behave when they know that the receiver had been unfair (skewed sharing) or fair (even sharing) in a similar game with another party. For example, in one version of such a game with no rights of rejection for the receiver, say one of the allocators, X, had kept Rs 98 for himself and allocated only Rs 2, while another allocator, Y, had split the amount equally, 50–50 with the receiver. A subject of the experiment is asked to choose one of the following two offers:

a. He is provided with a capital of Rs 90, of which he will keep Rs 45 for himself and give Rs 45 to Y, or
b. He is provided with a capital of Rs 100, of which he will keep Rs 50 for himself and give Rs 50 to X.

It has been frequently found in studies elsewhere that subjects prefer the first option, which rewards the fair guy, Y, rather than the unfair guy, X, even though the option entails taking a cut of Rs 5 for the subject.

Do Indians show a tendency to penalize the unfair, particularly when penalizing the unfair involves a cost to oneself? It appears not. Recall our discussion earlier regarding questions A6 and B6. We said that even when a vegetable vendor has been unfair to us, or a grocer runs an unkempt shop, we are not always willing to pay a price to penalize them. When we abet such behaviour by patronizing the unfair traders, we end up encouraging similar behaviour all over, which results in exploitation and ugliness all around. What appeared to be a D–C (or C–C) behaviour at a personal level turns out to be a D–D behaviour when viewed from a collective perspective. This is because patronizing such vendors may be viewed as cooperation from the vendor's perspective but a defecting behaviour from a societal perspective since patronizing such vendors leads to a nationwide malaise.

On the occasions I have conducted similar experiments in India and elsewhere, I have found a lower degree of self-regulation and disposition to sharing and a greater propensity and tolerance for unfairness among us Indians compared to the cosmopolitan average.

THE WAY WE ARE

Our lack of self-regulation has serious implications. Our Constitution, at the time of its conception and drafting, contemplated a democracy where the government was meant to serve the people. To achieve this, government was to be divided into three branches—legislature, judiciary and the executive—with each branch being able to supervise and regulate the other two. This was intended to be a system of checks and balances. In India, increasingly, each of these branches is striving to act in isolation, free from the influence or control of the other two. Often this leads to a situation where the judiciary begins to play an activist role. Once an issue is viewed as 'parliament versus judiciary', it provides leeway for various people to disregard the directions even of the highest court of the country. Only a few months ago, the Supreme Court had to order the eviction of a Governor of a state from a house that he was occupying in Delhi! The same Governor was also severely indicted by the Supreme Court for misleading the executive about the condition of polity in his state. According to news reports, rather than stepping down in a dignified manner, the Governor announced his intentions to 'take the salute' on Republic Day as the head of the state. In short, given the virtual non-existence of self-regulation among us as a people and given that it is people like us who populate each one of these three branches, there is bound to be an effect on the institutions as well. There is little surprise that the quality of our polity, bureaucracy and judiciary has declined.

I said earlier that our intelligence level is perhaps second to none in the world. Why then do we seem to lack self-regulation more than most other people in the world? Why are we reluctant to punish the unfair? What prevents us from seeing that, even if we are supremely selfish, it is in our best interest to cooperate? Let me hypothesize a couple of answers to these questions.

Firstly, as we ourselves are unfair to varying degrees it does not shock us when we encounter unfairness in others. This is apparent in the Indian response patterns to some of the questions relating to fairness and unfairness discussed earlier.

Secondly, there is little doubt that we are far more quick-witted than most others the world over. But our intelligence seems to be in the nature of rapid-fire intelligence, like that required in a rapid-chess tournament! For example, it is obvious to the rapid-thinking Indian corporates that it is not worthwhile to invest in research and development (R&D). Let someone else develop the product and it can always be copied. They earn some quick temptation points when they steer clear of such 'pointless' expenses as R&D except when it comes to claiming 100 per cent depreciation benefits for air conditioners and such in the R&D centres. As a consequence, in the long haul, our corporates are rarely world class and are not half as smart as they look in the short haul.

But intelligence isn't all about quick returns. For well-functioning societies, the intelligence required among people is the kind required in standard chess, which calls for thinking two, three or even more levels beyond, and not the kind required in lightning chess, where one barely gets to think one move ahead. Thus enlightened societies need to think of self-interest on the secondary, tertiary or even higher planes and not as instant gratification. One not only needs to strategize one's own game plan several moves ahead but one also needs to anticipate others' moves to each one of one's own, by putting oneself in the other's shoes. This we invariably fail to do.

WE MISTAKE TALK FOR ACTION

We are glib with our words. Not for nothing does Amartya Sen dub us the 'Argumentative' Indian(s). We can rationalize almost anything with verbiage. We are great debaters. We are also a complex people. The world perceives us so.

More often than not, we mistake talk for action, we mistake meetings held for decisions taken, reports written for action taken, judgement announced for judgement implemented, testimonials written for character assessed, speeches made for promises kept . . .

We preach democratic rights to the world but fail to provide basic quality of life to our masses; we take the moral high ground on any issue, but violate the basic rights of our own people to justice; we talk of equality before the world, but apply different yardsticks to our big crooks and small crooks; we talk of being the world's call centre, but do nothing for the children in the government-run schools and universities to ensure they learn English; we want a permanent seat in the UN Security

Council, but run our country like a fiefdom of a handful of politicians.

WE BRAZEN IT OUT

There is another related tendency of ours as a people that has indirect parallel with the observations just made. Elsewhere in the world, media reports seem to indicate that when people are presented with incontrovertible evidence of their misdeeds, after putting up some initial fight, they weaken, waver, give in and confess and show a degree of repentance. But closer home, our sense of shame and dishonour, if any, obtains not so much from the commission of the misdeed but from the exposure of it. You catch me with my hands in the till, and I'll look up innocently and ask you, 'What till?' We put up our best fights when we are up the proverbial creek—paddle or no paddle. If we are rich, powerful and famous, more often than not, we dock home safely. Videotape and cellphone evidence is rubbished with a straight face. BMWs driven by the offspring of the high and mighty that mow down half a dozen innocents simply disappear. A suitcase full of hot cash pulled out from under the bed of a powerful satrap can be allowed to go cold till public memory fades away. A supremo may be all but indicted in the highest court, and in exemplary punishment asked to 'introspect' on her sins. Witnesses may switch testimonies like a toggle switch. VVIPs may be repeatedly ordered by courts to vacate their illegally occupied bungalows to no effect. All this, because we neither regulate nor self-regulate; we neither penalize wrongdoers ourselves, nor do we expect our judiciary to do so.

DIFFERENT DEMOCRATIC YARDSTICKS

In India once a person attains a position of power, wealth and fame, no matter how much of a lowlife he is, he considers himself above the law and it is only when others in comparable positions have their own vested interest to bring him to book that he may show more respect for it. We do have such 'victims' screaming 'political motivation, harassment and witch-hunting by vested interests'. Such an accusation may well be true. But it may be equally true that but for such 'motivation' the lowlife would have got away completely without ever having to answer the law. All said, in reality, nothing ever happens since these are battles between 'heavyweights' who only end up sorting out their differences and finally settle the matter among themselves with some help from clever lawyers. That our judicial system itself is among the most ineffective in the world, and investigating agencies among the most bungling, indifferent and corrupt, helps. Little wonder that our heavyweights have nothing but disdain for our institutions of law and justice.

Here is an example. In a recent high-profile case, a high-flying personage was reportedly airlifted by a police posse on a small chartered plane from one city to another to effect an arrest on murder charges. The point raised by the hotshot legal counsel of the hotshot accused was how could the police carry their arms on a plane without clearance from the International Airports Authority! In this legal luminary's eyes, it was the police that was the villain on trial and not the murder accused. Clearly, the lawyer here was viewing the law as his handmaiden.

LONG-WINDED ARGUMENTS

The British courts boast of one of the shortest petitions ever.
A man had run his car into another, causing damage. The
matter went to court. The prosecution established the guilt of
the defendant and claimed a certain sum in compensation.
The defendant in his petition responded in four words:
'Liability accepted; compensation challenged!'

Imagine a typical Indian affidavit in a similar situation. It
may deny that an accident ever took place. It may argue that
the accident could not have taken place because the defendant
was not even in town on the day of the accident; or that the
accused did not ever own a car or a driving licence; or that he
had since changed his name or sex, while the petition had been
filed in the old name or sex, and hence was untenable. Each of
these points would be filed as a separate affidavit, one after
the other, with each affidavit requiring a few dozen
adjournments. In short, we would make the case so long-
winded, both in terms of paper and time, that a short and crisp
judgement becomes impossible. Given the way petitions are
heaped up in our courts, it is a miracle that a case ever comes
up for judgement.

If you think I'm merely exaggerating, consider the following
news item:[3]

In a major twist to her flip flops, Best Bakery case witness
Zahira Sheikh has told the Supreme Court that no
affidavit sworn by her was filed in the apex court based
on which the trial was shifted from Gujarat to Mumbai
and acquittal of the 21 accused quashed.

Zahira's latest affidavit came in response to the Supreme Court notice to her on an application filed by Teesta Setalvad seeking CBI probe into her recent shift of stand in the Bakery case accusing the social activist of pressurizing her to implicate persons in the case.

It is clear that Zahira has merely been a puppet in the hands of certain vested interests. But look at the issues raised. The Supreme Court had to decide if Zahira's change in stance amounted to contempt of court. But before the Court can proceed any further on the matter of contempt of court, which itself was the sub-agenda arising from the main case, the sub-sub-agenda of whether or not she had filed that affidavit will have to be decided first. This implies that, before the Supreme Court can give a final decision on the original Best Bakery case, it first has to establish that Zahira had filed the affidavit which led to the case being transferred outside Gujarat, and then on the strength of that case, decide whether or not there was contempt of court. Thus, where the Supreme Court had one case on hand, it now has three different cases. Is it any surprise that judgements take such a long-winded course?

To give one more example: the *Times of India* (31 December 2004) reported that Sunil Dutt, then Union minister for sports and youth affairs, could not identify the taxi driver accused of rash driving in a case dating back twenty years. Apparently, on 12 July 1984 Sunil Dutt and his companions were driving down 17th Road, Khar, when a taxi driver overtook their car rashly and even threatened to kill Dutt for warning him. After twenty years, when Dutt was asked to identify the driver, he refused as his conscience did not let him do what he was not sure about.

Surely we are a grand democracy of defections. Our guilty are free to defect against the spirit of the judiciary through innumerable adjournments; our municipalities are free to defect by letting our towns become seething ghettos; our politicians are free to defect taking democracy for a ride; our civil servants are free to defect just serving time; our universities are free to defect not carrying out any research or quality teaching; our judicial system is free to defect not dispensing timely justice; and we as a people are free to defect driving on the right-hand side of the road and spitting into each other's eyes. When the returning defections complete the D–D loop, we have a reverberating and throbbing India, a *functioning anarchy*, as Bertrand Russell called us.

Let us move on to the flip side of self-regulation, namely, free riding.

CHAPTER 7

Are We the World's Biggest Free Riders?

There is a parable about an ancient Indian king. He couldn't sleep worrying about the integrity of his subjects. So he decided to test them out, once and for all, to cure himself of insomnia. He proclaimed to all his subjects that he wanted each one of them to pour a glass of milk into a large cauldron kept at the town centre that night. The cover of darkness was to allay fears that the contents would be monitored as people poured the glass of milk into the receptacle. The next morning the king went to inspect the contents, only to find the vessel full of crystal clear water. Clearly, each of the subjects thought his or her glass of water would go unnoticed in a cauldron full of milk contributed by the others.

FREE RIDING AT A GALLOP

What our ancient king witnessed was the problem of free riding in action, or what Garrett Hardin called the Tragedy of the Commons.[1]

Free riding or Tragedy of the Commons is a problem not unique to us, Indians. Wherever there is public good, there are bound to be free riders. What do we mean by public good? Thaler offers a good definition.[2] According to him, a public good has the following two properties:

1. Once it is provided to one, it is costless to provide it to everyone else.
2. It is difficult to prevent one who doesn't pay for the good from using it.

Typical examples of 'public good' are the public radio and television, internet, non-toll highways, bridges, parks, temples, canals, sidewalks and village commons. When there is public good, there are bound to be those who will free ride. Free riders, even if they enjoy the benefits of the public good, will not pay for it because there is no 'rational' reason why they should.

Yet, not everybody free rides. Many of us do pay our taxes even if we could probably get away without having to; many of us do contribute to charities; and probably in real life that king would have found a feeble white solution in the cauldron, since there are always some who pay up for a variety of motives.

FREE-RIDING EXPERIMENTS

Behavioural researchers such as Thaler, Oliver and Mark,[3] among others, have done much work trying to find out why people do or do not free ride. The works include some delightful experiments, many of which I have enjoyed replicating for MBA students in India and abroad.

You too can replicate some of Thaler's experiments at your next party. Let's say you have ten guests. Give Rs 100 (real or notional) to each one of them. Tell them that they may either keep the money for themselves or contribute it to a common corpus. Tell them that the money contributed into the common kitty will be multiplied by a certain factor that is greater than one, but less than the number of participants, say, two. This multiplication simulates the fact that when contribution is made to public good, the government typically adds to that kitty, enhancing the kitty available for the greater good of all. You then tell them that for each participant contributing his Rs 100 to the corpus, you will double the amount and distribute it equally among all the ten participants, irrespective of whether or not they contributed to the kitty. The information on who contributed and who did not may be kept a secret, replicating the fact that in real life free riders are not always exposed.

Obviously, if all the ten participants contribute Rs 100 to the kitty, everybody takes home Rs 200, as the contribution to the kitty is doubled and equally divided among all. The participants, as a whole, double their wealth from an initial principal of Rs 1000 to Rs 2000. On the other hand, suppose everybody except one of your guests contributed Rs 100 to the kitty, then all the nine contributors (or cooperators) go home with Rs 180 each, while the free rider or the defector takes home Rs 280. The total capital of the ten participants, as a whole, increases from Rs 1000 to Rs 1900, that is, Rs 100 short of the maximum possible. Similarly, if half of them contribute while the other half do not, the five contributors take home only Rs 100 while the five free riders pocket 200 each. The total capital of the ten participants in this case goes up from Rs 1000 to Rs 1500 only. In short, it is obvious that if one contributes nothing, while the others do, one is better off than the others. But the strategy of free riding ensures that the group, as a whole, does not prosper. Yet, to human nature in general and us Indians in particular, it appears very rational to free ride.

It's fun to watch the game unfold. You can also give the game many twists and turns like allowing participants to make partial or full contribution, keeping the responses opaque or transparent; playing the game just once or playing it over and over again, and having the contributions made in single stage or multiple stages.

SOME VARIATIONS

Here is one interesting variation. If a minimum of six of the ten participants contribute Rs 100 each to the common kitty, each of the participants will receive Rs 200. Which means the contributors will go home with Rs 200 each, while the non-contributors will go home with Rs 300 each. If the number of contributors falls short of six, nobody gets anything, so that the contributors lose their contribution, while the free riders get to keep their Rs 100. It is particularly interesting to observe if the response patterns change if you keep repeating the game time and again.

Mostly, such games are played with hypothetical money, so that the responses may or may not be similar to the responses that may be expected if the same game were played with real money. But games like these are often difficult to play with real money or, when played with real money, the amounts are typically too small to simulate realistic stakes. I have therefore played out this version of the experiment on several occasions substituting grade points for money when the participants were MBA students. You will be surprised how closely grade points mimic money. Like money, you prefer more grade points to less, you want more grade points than your neighbour, and you are willing to fight true and dirty to win more and more grade points.

In one session involving nineteen participants, when the same game was played five times, not even in one game did the number of contributors exceed six. The sheepish students repeatedly told me that while they really wanted to contribute, they 'knew' their colleagues 'well enough', so they chose to defect.

Typically in these games, any one individual is better off not contributing to the kitty, yet the group's good is maximized only if a minimum number of individuals contribute. Researchers have experimented with the above version of the game in various situations. For example, participants in a game may or may not be allowed to talk to one another. Results indicate that often allowing people to talk to one another improves contribution, but does not eliminate non-contribution altogether.

In yet another variation, experiments have been conducted by splitting the participants into two groups, say, of twelve individuals each. Exercises are conducted to ensure that each group develops its own identity. Then two clusters of twelve each are formed again, by drawing six members from each group. The same game is re-enacted and, in one of the clusters, the members are told that their kitty collections will go to six members of their original group playing within the cluster, while, in the second cluster, members are told that their kitty collections will go to their six colleagues from the original group, now playing in the other cluster. If people did not have group affiliations, one would expect no significant difference in free riding across these two groups. However, such is not usually the case, indicating that people tend to free ride less when they share a feeling of oneness with their associates. So perhaps, in a more patriotic people, the degree of free riding ought to be less.

An interesting portrayal of this phenomenon may be witnessed in our second-class unreserved train compartments. For instance, I would do everything possible to get into a compartment, and once I am in I would do everything possible to keep others out. Now, don't we prove that hypothesis true in every walk of our life?

GREED, FEAR AND US

Why is it that, often, in these experiments the minimum threshold of contributors is not achieved? Clearly, the forces of greed and fear are at work here. Greed arises out of the possibility of taking home Rs 300 instead of Rs 200 should enough participants contribute. Fear arises out of the possibility that one may lose his Rs 100, if enough participants do not contribute. Which of the two sentiments is the more dominant?

We can modify the experiment to eliminate greed by ensuring that everyone (contributors as well as non-contributors) gets to take home Rs 200, provided a minimum of six guests contribute to the common kitty. Thus no one takes home Rs 300. Similarly, fear may be eliminated by providing for a 'money-back guarantee', where the contributors get their Rs 100 back in case the number of contributors falls short of six. However, should the number of contributors equal six or more, the contributors take home Rs 200 and the free riders Rs 300.

Researchers have found in these versions of the game that, in general, greed more than fear leads to free riding. For instance, Richard Thaler finds that while in the standard version the contributors averaged 51 per cent, in the no-fear version the contributors increased to 58 per cent, while in the no-greed version the contributors increased to 87 per cent. For corresponding Indian population, my limited and ad hoc experiments show these percentages to be around 30 per cent, 45 per cent and 85 per cent respectively.

Worldwide, in similar experiments, researchers have found 40 to 60 per cent of the respondents contributing to the kitty. For the Indian MBA student population, the percentage of contributors is closer to 35 per cent on an average. Could it be that, as a people, we Indians have a greater percentage of free riders? This is a hypothesis that needs rigorous testing.

SOME PRACTICAL IMPLICATIONS

From time to time, we hear of a company being bought out by employees or a portion of a company being restructured as an employee cooperative, with rewards based on the production of the unit. Leon Felkins says such arrangements do not always increase production dramatically.[4] This is because each employee in such an arrangement finds himself in a 'Commons' situation with the usual reward for freeloading. Unless the free-riding phenomenon is controlled, production is more likely to go down than up. We see the same phenomenon in our larger housing cooperatives, where free riding abounds. Tenants routinely modify their apartments at will, refuse to pay maintenance charges and misuse the common facilities. As such cooperatives are not hierarchical in nature, when combined with our weak self-regulation, the incentive to free ride is high.

HOW MUCH DO WE FREE RIDE?

The enormous size of our bureaucracy and the concomitant anonymity offer the most conducive environment for free riding. No wonder we see a horde of government employees idling, knitting, chatting or free riding their time away in any number of government departments. What little work gets done in such departments is done by a very small minority of workers, and the overall efficiency and effectiveness of our governmental system remain abysmally poor.

A smaller, hierarchical organization probably reduces the extent of free riding in a system. It is not surprising then that in the smaller private-sector organizations we see relatively less free riding. The reasons are simple. In a vast governmental bureaucracy, the fear of being caught free riding is very low. Hence the greed to benefit as much as possible is very high. In a smaller, private organization, the reverse is true, and hence free riding is much less.

A large organization, even when hierarchical, is more or less flat at any given level as each level has a huge number of employees, thereby being more conducive for free riding. Typically, this is not the case with smaller private organizations.

FROM FREE RIDING TO CORRUPTION

From free riding to corruption is but one step. As the probability of discovery goes down and greed increases constantly, the tendency to free ride graduates to corruption. Little wonder we rank among the most corrupt countries in the world in most world surveys. Some estimates put the proportion of graft in government contracts between 30 and 40 per cent.

Corruption is so widespread in every aspect of the bureaucracy and so specialized that there is a whole book on the manipulation of transfers by Indian bureaucrats.[5] The world-renowned Hoover Institution has an essay on India, 'India: Asia's Next Tiger?' by Hilton L. Root on their website, which is indeed insightful: Root writes:

> Where departments allocate licenses, subsidize goods, or raise money by black market sales (i.e., transport, public health, civil supplies, the development authority for land and projects), posts can command a good price. Power

over postings, therefore, is a key to understanding corruption.

Of late there has been much excitement among the masses regarding the bold sting operations by some TV channels, exposing some government officials and politicians accepting bribes. But then, exceptions apart, being caught on the tape can hardly jeopardize one's job or career, if one is resolute and can find someone else to bribe suitably.

Let us look at whether or not we are a systems-driven country and, if not, why?

CHAPTER 8

Systemic Chaos

India is a functioning anarchy.

—Bertrand Russell
(Philosopher and US Ambassador to India, 1962)

WE NEITHER IMPLEMENT NOR FOLLOW SYSTEMS

We talked about our lack of self-regulation arising from our proclivity for large-scale defect–defect behaviour. This lack of self-regulation also, at least partially, explains why we are not a systems-oriented nation. As we all know, we can create practically anything; only we cannot maintain what we create. We build airports, sports complexes, cinema halls, roads, bridges, parks and what have you, only to let them all go to seed for lack of maintenance. We practically run the nation without established systems. In fact, it would appear that we are fundamentally incapable of respecting or following systems. One government, one chief minister, one chief executive, or one head of the department may create a certain system but, even before that system is implemented, it is changed by the successor. A change itself would not be bad provided the change were for the better, but our changes are more in the nature of arbitrary negation of the functioning system. It is as if we are afraid or reluctant to allow the predecessor's systems work lest he gets the credit. In a way, our refusal to follow any system derives from our large-scale defection in the iterative PD situation.

ANATOMY OF SYSTEMS

No system can be foolproof. Every system of acceptance or rejection has two kinds of errors: Type 1 and Type 2. The first pertains to the possibility that an unworthy individual will pass muster in an examination or a defective product will pass quality control or a substandard service will be found acceptable. The second pertains to the likelihood that a worthy candidate will not make the grade or that a perfectly good product or service will be rejected. The best of systems cannot be foolproof against either kind of errors. They can only minimize them, unless one is willing to pay an enormous price.

If a system throws up one or the other error very often, clearly the system needs a review. But even when a system is fairly robust, one cannot rule out the two errors rising occasionally. The critical question is: When a system throws up an odd decision which suffers from one of the two errors, what should our course of action be? There are three options: a) In our belief that we have a sound system in place, we may accept that odd error as a one-off error, not warranting a change in the system per se; b) we may accept that particular decision, but look at ways to strengthening our system further so that such errors are further minimized in the future; or c) we may completely disregard the system and arbitrarily 'correct' the decision by reversing it, without doing anything to correct the system.

In case of 'a' or 'b', the integrity of a system that we believed to be fairly robust is respected. But what about alternative 'c'? This course of action not only demoralizes or discredits the current system, it also destroys the foundation for any system at all and, what is more, it increases both kinds of errors in due course and hence amounts to a defect type of decision. This is exactly the course we most often pursue.

ITC vs. Union Government

Take the issue of ITC, which won a case in the Supreme Court against the Union government, where the Supreme Court asked the government to refund Rs 350 crore collected by it in 1996 as a pre-deposit to ITC. What did the government do? Rather than accept the verdict of the country's own judicial system, it promulgated an ordinance in 2005 which in effect countermanded the verdict of the Supreme Court retrospectively. With this, the government could not only retain the Rs 350 crore, but force ITC to pay another Rs 450 crore (being the balance of an originally disputed amount of about Rs 800 crore) within a month or else pay penal interest. Sure this ensured the government temptation points of Rs 800 crore. But what it lost in the process is credibility. How will citizens, corporates and the rest of the civilized world believe that we have an effective judicial system, if judicial decisions are so easily reversible? The saga came to an end with the company signing a compromise with the government that enabled the latter to retain the pre-deposit money of Rs 350 crore in return for not pressing its claim for Rs 450 crore from the company.

Politicians on Academic Bodies

The second half of 2005 saw an upright vice chancellor of Bangalore University, in a rare intrepid display of intellectual integrity, rejecting five of the six candidates the state government had appointed to the university's syndicate, candidates who by no stretch of the imagination could be called educationists, eminent or otherwise. That the Karnataka government had the power to nominate so many of its hand-picked politicos into the senate was thanks to the State Universities Act 2000, which gave too much power to politicians to manage the universities in the state.

The high court quite rightly admonished the state government over its 'political nominations' and declared the nominations void. So what did the then state government do? It proposed to introduce a bill containing two amendments to the Karnataka State Universities Act 2000. One was to amend the section that required all the six nominees to be eminent educationists to one that merely required them to be 'anybody into education'. The section that restricted a nominee to a single term in the university's senate was amended to allow multiple terms.

What the judiciary held to be wrong in letter and spirit, the government was planning to introduce anyway. In short, we will create our democratic systems, but not follow them voluntarily.

Now let us look at the phenomenon from the prisoner's

dilemma perspective. When the government violates the spirit of the democratic system, it constitutes a major defection of sorts. And when you undermine the credibility of educational institutions thus, the society retaliates with a major defection of its own. How? It takes the form of marginalizing the graduates of such a university. In the 1970s and 1980s, for example, the colleges in Bangalore used to fiddle around (defect) with the university's examination system to award first class to students who had barely scrapped past their higher secondary examinations. The society retaliated with counter-defection. National advertisements for jobs added, 'Students from Bangalore University need not apply'. It took several years for the university to change that image.

The Sourav Ganguly Episode

Take the controversial dropping of Sourav Ganguly from the Indian cricket team in 2005. We have an apex cricketing body—the Board of Cricket Control in India (BCCI); we have a selection committee put together by the BCCI, presumably consisting of professionals; we have a high-profile coach, whom we went out of our way to woo and get. The selection committee, the coach and the captain of the team discussed the issue and decided to drop Ganguly.

Assume that the decision to drop Ganguly was a mistake of Type 1. So what did we do as a nation? We went by alternative 'c'. How? Everybody, from the BCCI president, the Lok Sabha Speaker, and the West Bengal chief minister to anybody who thought Sourav was 'Dada' to them, made it their business to force the selection committee to 'undo' this 'error'. Assuming for a moment that dropping Sourav was a Type-1 blunder (not just an error), are we to interpret that it was a serious systemic flaw? If we thought our selectors were unaware of Sourav Ganguly's Test batting average in his earlier matches, what can we say about the process that threw them up as selectors in the first place? And if there is nothing wrong with the selection committee, what is more important—the integrity of the Indian selection system or an individual? By reversing the decision, without changing anything in the system, what statement was made about the credibility of the selectors? How can we change a systemic decision so arbitrarily and yet expect to maintain the integrity of a system?

Tragically, we do accept such flouting of systems as a matter of course in every walk of life. What is worse, somewhere along the line our corruption and flouting of systems also get mixed up. Often they become the flip side of the same coin. For example, it may be a moot point to debate whether the various public service commissions or selection boards are merely flouting systems or are thoroughly corrupt. The same may be said about our constabulary system, land registration system, ration card system, pension system, or practically any 'system' in the country. In effect, we fail to see that a country of a billion people cannot be ruled with a billion different wills. We need systems like a newborn baby needs milk.

We do have a few instances of robust systems which clearly show the advantages of having strong systems in place. Take some of our institutions of higher learning such as the IITs and the IIMs. If undue influence cannot work to get a candidate through interviews in these institutions, it is thanks largely to the robust system that they have in place. That does not mean these processes never suffer from Type 1 and Type 2 errors. Occasionally, not-so-worthy candidates do get in, and some very worthy candidates do get left out. But these are systemic errors. These apart, because willy-nilly the institutional systems have been preserved, these centres have emerged as islands of excellence. Yet, we are nowhere ready to learn from the fruits of our own successful examples.

AND WHEN WE DO HAVE SYSTEMS

More often than not, our well-functioning systems are either informal, illegal or odd-ball systems. If they are legitimate, they are more likely to be applied neither intelligently nor equitably and hence are more or less defunct. These systems are often meant for the ease of application of the administrators rather than for the benefit of the users, customers or masses. More often than not, the systems are tiresome and completely devoid of sense as can be seen in the following examples.

We are a hot and sunny country. The temperature in summer can soar to over forty-five degree celsius in most states. Yet, I have rarely seen any of our municipal workers cleaning the streets by night, or our construction workers building roads and bridges by night, or our traffic squads painting the road lines or zebra crossings by night. Ideally, such an arrangement would make life much easier for the workers, for they can rest during the day when it is blistering hot and work at night when the temperature is a good six to eight degrees lower. The practice would also cause less obstruction to the traffic. Even in the coldest of the countries such activities are carried out by night. So why not in our country? What prevents us from creating systems that are more suited to our geography or climate?

Of the informal but durable systems, we have many. The dowry system is one such. The caste system is another. Our garbage disposal system (of simply throwing it in front of the house) is yet another. Our rural toilet system is no less robust. One could go on. These are systems that have come to stay forcefully.

But it is on our illegal systems that we actually thrive. Here are some examples.

Take the case of the demolition drive in Delhi in early 2006. How is it that we first allow illegal constructions to come up for decades, and then one fine morning wake up to the fact and wage a war on such structures overnight? Even when the drive is on, how come the properties of the powerful are rarely touched? It is not as if these deviations occur unknown to the authorities. But once these authorities receive their illegal gratification, any deviation is there to stay. For some reason, giving a bribe, particularly when you have no choice, appears to be less of a defection than taking it. But in reality, is it? Isn't it a collective thing? If there is no giver, there will be no taker. But who will take the initiative? Clearly, one can only begin with oneself and not another party; only then can the prisoner's dilemma problem be resolved.

Then, there is a wonderful system that operates in Mumbai providing 'insurance' for ticketless travel. It is (or at least was) a rather well-functioning system. If you pay your monthly premium to the 'insurers', you can travel ticketless in the suburban train. If you are caught (the probability of which is rather low) and fined (which is also relatively low as a proportion of the original fare when compared to the penal provisions in other countries), you simply produce the fine receipt before the 'insurers' and your fine amount is promptly refunded.

Clearly, the system works, since the insurance premium is much less than the monthly fare, and the probability of being caught and the consequence of it are both extremely low. What is more, the 'insurers' never 'defect' vis-à-vis their customers, as the regular insurance companies might do. One reason could be that the threat of your police complaint about any defection from the insurers can have relatively high adverse consequences for the ticketless travel insurer as compared to the legitimate insurers. The other reason could be you are less likely to 'defect' on the ticketless travel insurer—who may well be a local goon—by making a fake claim. If our illegal systems do work well, does it mean we are capable of operating efficient systems? I think not. We saw earlier that in an iterative PD situation, the idea is to maximize the overall satisfaction points and not win against others. But that is not how we see things. With us, it is always 'winning' against every other person we interact with, which a standardized system rarely permits.

The odd-ball systems, run rather efficiently, are very few.

THE ODD-BALL SYSTEMS

Of the rare but prevalent systems, the best example may be the service rendered by the Mumbai Topiwalas or Dabbawalas, who deliver lunch boxes to millions of people in Mumbai—come hell or high water—with an error rate of less than one wrong delivery per million. In the present-day management jargon it is referred to as a 6-sigma system.

Then we have the milk collection system created by Kurien through his milk-cooperative movement in Gujarat. That even the top business schools in the world should think of developing case studies on these systems, and that we are not able to replicate these experiences in practically any other ongoing system, is perhaps testimony, if one were needed, to how rare such well-functioning systems are in the Indian context.

Then there are odd-ball systems which are not ongoing as in a day-to-day sense. Our census survey held once a decade is one. The other is our voting system (on an average once in five years). Yet another is the system surrounding the Kumbh Mela (once in twelve years). Even our daily milk and newspaper supply systems are quite robust. Occasional hiccups and problems notwithstanding, these are among the best of our systems.

Finally, here are a few examples which happen to be first-hand observations of some of our legitimate, ongoing systems from the aviation sector alone.

Travelling on Indian Air

This is an example of a hare-brained 'system'. If you take one of the international flights of Indian Airlines (mostly to and from the Middle-East) to fly within the domestic sector, you will be given a slip at the check-in counter, which you have to fill up and hand over to the customs authorities sitting just after the emigration. The form asks you to declare that you do not possess watches, gold jewellery, TVs, diodes, zip fasteners, photographic cameras etc. 'of foreign origin' and Indian currency more than Rs 5000.

Let us quickly enumerate the absurdities of this process:

1. The form is meant to be filled up only by domestic passengers (flying within India). If so why should they declare their watches, TV sets, zip fasteners, etc. of foreign origin, when passengers flying by domestic flights do not have to do so? In other words, why is it all right for a domestic passenger to carry a TV or a watch of foreign origin as his baggage without a declaration if he is flying from Bangalore to Hyderabad by a domestic flight of Indian Airlines, but not so if the same passenger is flying the same route in an Indian Airlines flight going from Bangalore to Hyderabad to Sharjah?

2. And zip fasteners? Diodes? In this day and age?

3. Photographic camera? What other kinds of cameras are there anyway? And whatever happened to liberalization?

4. And Rs 5000 in cash, when any average credit card will enable one to draw five times that amount anywhere in a single day? Gold jewellery? But beyond how much value? Besides, in practically every domestic airport you can see the Airport Authority's signage allowing passengers to carry cash way above the absurd limit stated in the above form. So why this discrepancy between a domestic passenger travelling within the country on domestic flights and a domestic passenger travelling within the country on international flights?

To investigate if these questions really had some deeper

significance, I once diligently listed out my ipod, gluco-meter, pen-drive, gold cuff-links, Rs 5500 cash that I had carried that day on purpose and a spare imported watch. When the customs inspector saw my form, he was completely flummoxed. He asked me why I had listed out these items. When I pointed out that the form demanded my declaration, he had no clue on how to handle the situation. Finally, he gave me a new form, asking me to simply put nil against each item, and then let me pass.

Maybe there is some deep significance to the form and it serves some higher purpose apart from providing employment to hundreds of desultory customs inspectors in the country. But we may never know.

Vizag Airport and the Indian Airlines

Vishakapatnam has a relatively small airport. Alliance Air operates only old Boeings here. These aircraft have such small overhead luggage bins that even a standard hand baggage does not fit into them. The stewards repeatedly appeal to the passengers to shove their luggage under their seats. Often the bags are so large that shoving them under the seat is impossible. Finally they are deposited in the undercarriage, with a receipt given to every passenger. This delays the flights by a good thirty to forty minutes every time. Why can't passengers with large bags be asked to check in their bags beforehand rather than delay the flight? When asked, the flight crew typically wash their hands off the problem, saying that despite their repeated requests the ground-staff do not cooperate. Pose the question to the duty manager and he tells you the reason is non-cooperation of the Airports Authority security staff who refuse to filter hand baggage according to size. The security staff in turn say their job is simply to check the hand baggage from a security point of view—whether it fits into the aircraft or not is not their concern.

At the end of it, the problem remains unaddressed. All they need is a simple system in place. At the X-ray section, the Indian Airlines authorities could place a baggage frame suitable for the luggage rack of the old Boeings. Each passenger has to place the hand baggage in this frame; if the bag fits into that frame, it could be allowed as hand baggage. Surely, if there is a will to address this problem, it can be very easily addressed with no extra cost or work. Why can't we implement such a system?

Ahmedabad and Mumbai Terminals

Or consider this. Both Ahmedabad and Mumbai airports have newly refurbished terminals. Both are swanky with a lot of granite, glass and needlessly expensive yet tacky plaster-of-Paris false ceilings. Clearly cost containment has not been a major agenda. That is fine. The problem is that the Ahmedabad terminal provides for exactly one narrow entry-cum-exit door at the departures section. As hundreds of passengers push and shove their carts from that narrow entry, even as the airport staff is trying to push a train of luggage trolley out of the same gate, you have a perennial bedlam. A long queue begins to form, which continues to grow longer at the check-in counter and then the single X-ray machine. The old, the infirm, children and women with babies, all have to stand for almost an hour to gain entrance into the boarding area. Mumbai's new terminal has two security gates and two X-ray machines, but the problem remains largely unaddressed given that the passenger traffic is very high. This alone delays the outbound flight by at least half an hour.

Once again, why could we have not done a better systemic planning to avoid the bottlenecks? True, security at Indian airports is an issue of major concern. But should not passenger comfort be of equal concern? So why can't there be an array of security gates and X-rays? Surely, our systems, if any, are designed for the comfort of administrators and not their clients?

SELF-WORTH VS RULES

Our disregard for systems is reinforced when we see our VVIPS flouting the airport queues every day. We stand there for forty minutes, first at the security, then at the check-in counter and then at the X-ray machine. Along comes a politician or a civil servant who is simply whisked ahead of us. How come the basic systems, processes, rules, regulations and laws do not apply to them? How come most of us standing in the queues do not even fight for our right to be served first?

To Indians, in general, a position of power is synonymous with special privileges. The norms, systems and processes of the ordinary folk do not apply to the high and mighty. So deep-rooted is this belief that if a security guard so much as asks a man clad in spotless whites for his identity card, he stands to lose his job. 'Do you know who I am?' is a standard phrase employed to throw one's weight around in this country. In a Western country, so used are they to treating everyone as equal before the law that they actually do not understand the question or its implied threat. Many of our politicians have had a rude shock when faced with this reality abroad. Ours is a classic case of iterative PD in action. It is our politicians and other VIPs in the government who have conditioned the country into accepting different standards of rules, regulations and laws for those in power and for ordinary citizens. The law enforcer has been conditioned to bend before the ministerial power. He may not question when a white-clad man surrounded by four burly safari-clad men jumps queues at the airport security. He may not ask an important-looking man in a train for his ticket. He may not dare ask any occupant in a white Ambassador with a red light on the roof for his identity.

Of course the terrorists, having observed the situation well, used a white Ambassador (with red light of course) to enter the Parliament in December 2001, endangering the lives of the same ministers and babus who led them to their gatecrashing tactic, a sort of grand finale of 'defection begets defection' situation.

LACK OF STANDARDIZATION

Perhaps it is this lack of systems-orientation among us that ensures we are also a country without any standardization. Consider this. When you travel in other countries, you find their roads, shoulders, sidewalks, road signs, road dividers, speed breakers, etc. all so standardized that when you move from one province to the next, or one state to the other, you do not find much variation in these standards. You always know, more or less, what to expect. But in India, you can never be sure what to expect around the next corner. Leave alone across panchayats, provinces or states, even within a city there is little standardization. Our speed breakers come in all shapes and sizes and if they account for a disproportionately large percentage of all road accidents in India, it is nobody's concern. Our road signs, when they are there, are standardized neither in their content nor in their position and not even in their enforcement. Our vehicle number plates are tolerated in any language. Our road dividers could be anything ranging from slabs of stone or cement to tin barrels and plain boulders. Does this all tie up with prisoner's dilemma? The fact is that we need to cooperate first to standardize anything. This will, in turn, generate cooperation from the 'standardized' system, as it benefits all. But a defection on our part in not making that extra effort to standardize our systems begets defection by a huge non-standard ad hoc system.

OUR PROPENSITY TO LOOK FOR LOOPHOLES IN LAWS

Defection is our national trait. So also is looking for loopholes in practically every law or system. In fact much of the Indian legal system, particularly at higher levels, revolves around capitalizing on this trait. Be it our company law or criminal law, we thrive on finding loopholes in these laws.

If the government announces a higher interest income on fixed deposits for senior citizens, we would find hundreds of names, including those of family servants, their offspring and cousins, to make use of that provision. The same may be true for ration cards or a subsidy. Finding loopholes around income tax or various other taxes is of course too well known to merit enumeration. 'You show me a system, a law, a rule and I'll show you a couple of loopholes for each' is our credo. It requires a measure of self-regulation to recognize that the true role of lawyers is to pursue genuine prosecution, defence or advice under the ambit of the available legal provisions and not to get the crooks off the hook using legal loopholes in those provisions.

The iterative PD situation, as a consequence of large-scale defection, is there for all of us to see—a whole country full of defections—so full that our legal system barely works, with millions upon millions of long-wound cases piling up in our decrepit court houses.

Perhaps it is about time we addressed that poser termed as the 'Veerappan Dilemma' in the prologue.

CHAPTER 9

Veerappan Dilemma: The Poser Answered

We talked of the Veerappan Dilemma in the prologue and my poser was whether you saw any realistic chance of you or any of the other nineteen claimants getting that Rs 50-crore reward. 'Pretty unlikely,' you might have surmised after much deliberation.

Your argument on whether or not to write might have been as follows: 'If I do not write to the chief minister's office, I am not getting the award anyway. But if I write, there is always a chance, however minuscule, that the other nineteen are all by some chance posted in Antarctica, and do not receive the chief minister's letter in time. So I might as well write.'

So you write. And so do each one of the other nineteen, arguing exactly the same way. In all probability, the chief minister's office ends up receiving twenty identical notes, when a mere two would have sufficed to disqualify all the twenty from getting the award.

Now this is extremely frustrating. There does not seem to be any way for any of the twenty to win the award. If the chances are so minimal, you ought not to waste your time writing that letter. If a good many of the twenty think that way and choose not to waste their time, there is always a minute chance that one of the twenty decides to do otherwise and gets to be the lucky winner. It might as well be you. So you decide to write. So do the others, all for the same reason!

Also if you do not write, you do not qualify for the award anyway, and so you decide to write. But in doing so, you also kiss goodbye to any chance of laying your hands on the reward.

But wait a minute. Don't despair yet. Recall, I said that all the twenty shortlisted claimants are assumed to be very intelligent.

THE RESOLUTION

So let us say you arrive at the following resolution about whether or not to write that cursed letter claiming the reward.

'I will put twenty balls, numbered 1 to 20, into a bowl. I will mentally decide on a certain number between 1 and 20, say, number 5. I will give the bowl a good shake, and draw a ball blindfolded. I will then open my blindfold and read the number of the ball I drew. If this happens to be a number other than 5, I will not write the letter. But if the ball I drew is indeed number 5, I will write that letter. In short, I will write that letter with a probability of one in twenty and not write that letter with a probability of 19/20.'

Assume that each of the other nineteen claimants also makes an identical resolution.

Nineteen out of twenty chances are that you do not draw number 5 and hence, in accordance with your resolution, you will not write the letter claiming the reward. But resolutions are often for breaking. If you do not draw number 5, chances are you begin to argue with yourself along one of the following lines:

'Now that according to the accursed draw I am not supposed to write that stupid letter I am out of the reward anyway. Why should I leave it to any other bloke to get lucky? So let me write in any case!'

Or,

'Oh God, I should have drawn the ball with my right hand instead of my left. So let me draw again. And if this turns out to be a number other than 5 once again, I'll try one more time . . . third time final . . .'

You would 'cheat' against your resolution till you get a draw that suits you, that is, gets you to write, or you simply write anyway, chucking your resolution.

But if you are capable of such thinking or action, so are all the other nineteen. So very likely, nobody may be a respector of the resolution, and your reward remains elusive.

Assume that each one adheres to the resolution and does not cheat. Under this condition, you realize one of the twenty claimants might well end up getting that reward. The reason is based on simple probability.

The probability that any one claimant draws a ball with a specific pre-decided number and therefore gets to write is one in twenty. Since there are twenty claimants, the overall probability that only one of them will draw the pre-decided number and hence be the only one to write that letter is slightly under 38 per cent, a rather high probability, considering you did not see the faintest possibility of any claimant getting that award.[1]

In short, if each one followed the resolution honestly and steadfastly, the probability that one of the twenty claimants will get the award goes up to about two in five. It is like saying, if you scrupulously follow that resolution, you have bought into a lottery that gives a 38 per cent chance that one of the twenty claimants will win Rs 50 crore. That's a pretty good lottery.

SHRÖDINGER'S CAT

Yet, how many of us are capable of sticking to a resolution? Don't we typically wonder, 'How is my action related to others' actions? Aren't our actions entirely independent of each other, just like my drawing a number from my jar is independent of others drawing the numbers from theirs? If so, and if all the rest are sticking to their resolutions, am I not better off departing from the resolution and writing that letter anyway? I certainly can't be worse off doing that? Obviously what I do or do not do cannot influence the others?'

Your action may be independent of the others', but what reason do you have to believe that others will not think the way you do? Others too would have reasoned similarly and dispatched their letters posthaste, ensuring no one got that award. In a way, everybody's actions are independent and yet dependent at the same time; just like light is both a particle and a wave at the same time; or like Shrödinger's Cat[2] which is both alive and dead at the same time.

Yet, this quantum-mechanics-like dilemma hides a fundamental and absolute truth, namely, if everyone scrupulously follows that resolution, you (and for that matter everyone) stand a pretty good chance of getting that big booty; but if you cheat, it is curtains down on a big fortune. That is why the right conduct is to be internally driven not externally driven. 'Am I doing the right thing?' is the only relevant question. That 'others may cheat' is irrelevant. That route of questioning never resolves the PD-like dilemma.

VEERAPPAN DILEMMA COMPOUNDED

Assume that the chief minister of the neighbouring state doubles the stake and announces a Rs 100-crore award to those who helped in trapping Veerappan. This state too has a large number of claimants for the award. In fact, the numbers are soaring so high that the chief minister, in a bid to pre-empt the rush, has thrown open the award to the entire state with a population of some ten crore.

The format of the chief minister's announcement is somewhat different from that of the first state. This format announces the total reward money to be Rs 100 crore/N for each claimant, where N is the total number of claims received by the chief minister's office. The chief minister also adds there is no reason why an individual should be restricted to a single claim, given that people's abilities can vary widely from one to another. So each subject of the state is allowed up to a thousand claims. But other terms remain more or less the same as in the first state, such as 'If you don't send in your note, you don't qualify for the reward,' etc.

But the state government is eco-friendly and does not want to waste too much paper on multiple claims. It asks its subjects to use a format similar to that used by the other state except that it provides a small box at the top right-hand corner of the note, where one could merely write the total number of claims one was tendering, as indicated below:

Your address:

No. of Claims:

Yes, I would like to receive my share of the award of Rs 100 crore only (Rupees One Hundred Crore Only) for the valiant role I played in helping to bring about the untimely demise of Late Sri Munusamy Veerappan.

Yours Faithfully

Signature

Your name:
Dated:

If yours is the only note that the chief minister's office receives and you decide to send in a single claim, you could pocket the entire sum as your reward as in that case N will be 1. Little chance though. In fact you will be lucky if each resident sends in one claim each, so that you land a tenner (Rs 100 crore/ 10 crore). More likely, each citizen will tender the maximum entitlement of 1000 claims which means you will more likely take home barely over one paisa on your single claim. So there is no way you are going to make a single claim. You, like all the others, reason it is better to make the maximum number of claims possible, 1000. So whether the entire population of the state sends a single claim each or 1000 claims each the result is one and the same.

Do you think there is any reasonable chance of any one individual winning the entire reward? Well, it is not as bad as it looks. In fact your chances are far better than in a lottery. Let us reason as follows:

If each citizen independently resolves to throw a ten-crore-sided die (or uses a random number generator) and sends in one claim with a probability of one in 10,00,00,000 and does not send any claim with a probability of 9,99,99,999 in 10,00,00,000, there is still approximately 37 per cent $[(9,99,99,999/10,00,00,000)^{9,99,99,999}]$ chance that one of the ten crore citizens will get the entire Rs 100 crore! But resolutions are known to be weak universally. If only we knew what weak resolutions can cost!

As you will notice, the Veerappan Dilemma is quite similar to the prisoner's dilemma, in that it is like a multipeople one-time prisoner's dilemma and the logic for everyone is as symmetrical in this poser as it is in the case of one-time prisoner's dilemma. There are no opportunities for the participants to learn through repeated iterations. In fact, many of our collective behaviour issues raised in some of the last few chapters fall under this category. Imagine, if only we, as an entire people, had the necessary resolve in our character to invest, say, in a rainwater collection and recharge system in our backyard, because that is the correct thing to do, our national water shortage problem could get solved. Of course as a free loader I may be better off not investing my money and yet benefit from the rising water table, thanks to the actions of the others. But if I think that way, Schrodinger's Cat tells me that is what everybody else may be thinking, and our water table may never rise!

CHAPTER 10

Game Theory and the Gita

A jawan is posted to Kargil, where the battle is on. He faces a dilemma. If he proceeds to Kargil, he may end up paying the highest price—his life—thus leaving his young wife and children destitute. If he refuses to go, he may face humiliation and possibly a jail sentence for desertion or dereliction of duty. Still it is a rational choice as the price he has to pay for desertion is negligible when compared to losing one's life and leaving one's family destitute. Yet, he proceeds to the battlefront, like all other jawans. One wonders if any jawan even considers the situation as a dilemma. He simply does what he considers is his duty, his dharma.

I am not religious, at least not in the conventional sense of the term. Nor am I well-versed in any of the religious scriptures, the Bhagavad Gita included. My understanding of religions and scriptures is simple: all religions are fundamentally noble; none asks you to do wrong; each religion has tolerance towards your sins; all of them have a good dose of fiction in the form of some really far-flung mythological stories, many of them truly spectacular and entertaining, not unlike *The Lord of the Rings . . .*

Like most simple folk, my early view of god was shaped by what I observed around me. Going by this observation, god was like a petty government official. It was clear to me that god, like the government babu, needs to be kept in good humour by periodic offerings and promises of this and that; that he needs some inducement if I want him to do something for me—and the bigger my wish the bigger will have to be the inducement offered; that it is better to wait and see if he does his bit, before I keep my bargain; that, if he did his bit and I did not keep my bargain, he will come after me for recovery with threats of dire consequences in this life or the next; that he has a healthy appetite and takes umbrage if you eat ahead of him, and so forth.

I also learnt that god is not without his sadistic side, so that in lieu of material inducements, you could also compensate him by animal sacrifices or some masochistic acts of your own, such as starving yourself sick or torturing yourself cruel.

This idea of god shaped my attitude towards practising religions, which naturally was not very positive. So what am I doing, writing a chapter on the Gita? Till a few years ago, all I knew about the Gita was half a sloka, which was:

Karmanyavädhikarastey mä faleshu kadächanä

Meaning:
You have right only to the action and never to the fruit
of the action.

I did not know for quite some time that this was not a
canto in itself but had a second half to it:

Karmanyavädhikarastey mä faleshu kadächanä
Ma karmafalheturbhurmä te sango sthvakarmni
$\qquad$ Bhagavad Gita, Chapter II, Verse 47
Meaning:
You have right only to the action and never to the fruit
of the action.
Fruit of action should not be your motivation, nor should
you be driven by attachment to action.

For most of my youth and a little beyond, I always found these
words innocuous and naive. Taking this bit of verse as a
random sample of what the Gita was all about, I thought I
understood why we weren't a result-driven people. You see,
innocence can lead to such quick generalizations.

Meanwhile, a good Samaritan presented me a copy of the
Gita, which I did read now and then, though rarely pausing to
contemplate seriously on its contents.

It was only when I started getting interested in game theory
and immersed myself in it that the whole import of the Gita
hit me like a truck.

In many ways, the Gita, in a quintessential form, lays down what one may call the absolute truth for most aspects of our lives, the dharma. To amplify this statement further: for years, my idea of right and wrong was largely intuitive. Yet somewhere deep down, I could never see any reasonable evidence to believe that there existed absolute truths outside physical sciences which one could 'measure and prove'.

My argument was: If this is a world of 'selfish genes' and therefore selfish people, what makes it 'wrong' to shaft somebody, as long as you found it worth your while? Religions may proscribe shafting somebody, pronouncing such action as a sin. But the question is: 'Why is it a sin?' Who is to say that a wrong has happened, given that each individual is selfish and each one's actions are supposed to be in the best interests of oneself? Similarly, the Gita might say that it is wrong to be driven by desires. But why is it wrong? Again, if I see a child begging for alms at a traffic crossing, what is the correct course of action? To give alms and risk reinforcing the system, or desist and risk the child going hungry? Which is the lesser evil?

For questions such as these and other social dilemmas, there don't seem to be answers that are right or wrong. Or so I had believed for a long time. I was enlightened when I found game theory capable of answering many questions such as these unambiguously. But what really captured my imagination was that most answers which a game-theoretic situation such as prisoner's dilemma yielded were consistent with what Krishna had to say to Arjuna in the Bhagavad Gita! I discovered that modern game theory and associated experiments and games seem to validate what Krishna had placed before Arjuna in a nutshell. Clearly, it took thousands of years for management science to validate the Gita (even if unwittingly), much as present-day experiments on the outer reaches of space continue to validate Albert Einstein.

Let me demonstrate how we may attempt to understand the Gita via game theory.

Consider our simple prisoner's dilemma situation of Chapter 4. For either of us on the horns of the prisoner's dilemma, there is one path, namely cooperation, which if we both follow, leads to a total prison sentence of four years (two years each), while the other paths entail a total sentence of five years (none for the defector and five years for the cooperator when one of the two defects) or eight years (four years each when both defect).

Hence, for the two accomplices, cooperation must be the correct course of action or the dharma, as it entails their larger good. If so, defection must be adharma (or betrayal of duty) as it collectively entails a greater sentence of five or eight years, against cooperation that entails only four years. In fact, the more the adharma in the society (both defecting amounting to 'more' adharma than only one of the two defecting), the more the collective suffering (eight years collectively versus five years).

Krishna also says:

Yogastha kuru karmani sangtyaktvä Dhananjya
Sidhyasidhyo samo bhutvä samatvam yoga uchate
                              Bhagavad Gita, Chapter II, Verse 48

Meaning:
Immersed in yoga, conduct action without attachment,
O conqueror of wealth (Arjuna);
Staying even-minded (objective or balanced) in success
and failure; such equanimity is called yoga.

This equanimity is called for in prisoner's dilemma. If at the
verge of doing the right thing, that is, taking the decision to
cooperate, one keeps an eye on the possibility that the other
may defect causing 'loss' to oneself, one is no longer
committing oneself to action without attachment. One is no
longer in a state of equanimity between success (C–C situation)
and failure (C–D situation). If one is a true karmayogi, one
just does the right thing, that is, cooperate, and moves on,
irrespective of what the other might do.

If you do that, continues Krishna:

Tasmädhasttha säthatham karyä karma samächar
Asattho hyacharnkarma parmäpnoti purusha
                    Bhagavad Gita, Chapter III, Verse 19
Meaning:
Thus, being forever unattached, execute action that needs
to be executed;
Certainly working without any attachment, the righteous
man achieves the highest good.

If everyone followed the path of the karmayogi stipulated by
the Gita, C–C is the only outcome and that leads to the 'highest
good'.

Krishna's advice on controlling desire is apt in the context of controlling the temptation that prisoner's dilemma offers. Says Krishna, in repeated exhortations to Arjuna:

Tasmatvmindriyanyädow niyamya bharatarshabh
Päpmanam prajahi hyon jnanavigyananäshanam
Bhagavad Gita, Chapter III, Verse 41

Evam budhe param budhhvä sansatbhyatmänamätmanä
Jahi shatrum mahäbäho kämarupam duräsadam
Bhagavad Gita, Chapter III, Verse 43

Yasya sarvey samärambhä kämasankalpavarjitä
Jnanagnidagdhkarmänam tamähu panditam budhä
Bhagavad Gita, Chapter IV, Verse 19

Meaning:
Thus, O the best of Bharatas (Arjuna), contain these senses (and)
Shed away this desire which is the destroyer of wisdom and knowledge
And knowing that Self is higher than the intellect and controlling yourself by the Self;
O mightily armed one (Arjuna), crush your desire which is your unassailable enemy.
One whose actions are free from desire and self-seeking purpose; and
One whose actions are fired by wisdom—he is called wise by the learned.

It is clear that, in prisoner's dilemma, the root of the evil is the temptation that leads to the D–D decision. By controlling one's desire or temptation, and taking that action which is fired by wisdom, we show ourselves to be wise and achieve the highest good.

One can see here that at a deeper level, Krishna's words concerning selflessness are not about renunciation of all that is good and enjoyable. Rather, it puts the means above the end and says that, if your means or actions are just and honourable, the end takes care of itself. This is true, as we have seen in prisoner's dilemma. If end alone tempts you, and if end alone fires your desire, you are bound to commit actions that do not ensure the end you are striving to achieve. This too is true of prisoner's dilemma!

Metaphorically then, not to open your water taps fully while shaving is dharma; not to jump the red light on the traffic signal is dharma; and not to pollute the air we breathe is dharma. By the same token, in the context of the Veerappan Dilemma, writing the letter to the chief minister in accordance with the resolution we talked about is dharma. Similarly, cheating on the draw and writing the letter is adharma. Clearly, if everybody follows the path of dharma, water becomes abundant; the traffic flows smooth; the air becomes breathable; and the award winnable.

That is why we must not 'defect'; that is why those who do not follow the path of dharma ought to be punished; that is why it is one's dharma to be provoked by the adharmi and retaliate, and yet show compassion and forgiveness in the conduct of one's actions, just as the Tit for Tat strategy guides us.

This is what game theory tells us, and this is what the Gita tells us as well. It is just that the Gita is a simplified and made-easy or ready-to-serve version of actions that the game theory plods through to demonstrate. It is interesting that some sage, aeons ago, thought of the right courses of action for humanity at large in a variety of situations that can stand the test of proof of present-day tools and techniques, including computer simulation.

But I must hasten to add a word of caution here. I have shown how, as supported by game theory, it pays to follow the dharma, or the right conduct.

But I am not well-versed in the Gita. Nor am I sure if I subscribe to all references to dharma, for instance, those pertaining to the caste system. I shall therefore desist from holding forth on this somewhat fascinating territory any further. My intention in writing this chapter was merely to share my own personal awakening to many aspects of the Gita. What is strange is that we should be witnessing so much of defect–defect behaviour in the very land that gave us the Gita. Clearly, while the West, using its cumbersome vehicle of game theory, has covered a lot of ground in collective cooperative behaviour, we seem to have made very little headway in that direction, notwithstanding our heritage of the Gita.

Epilogue

58 Summers after Independence

If we can launch rockets but get nowhere,
Fire missiles, but not our passions to excel,
Build aircraft but cannot fly our dreams;

If we can build oil rigs, cyclotrons and atomic plants,
but not our character,
Make heavy machinery and earth-moving equipment,
Yet not move heaven and earth to improve our fate;

If we can grow enough grain, but not care enough
to store them,
Allow half our population to go hungry, with
malnutrition and ill-health still our national visage;

If our population is well over a billion, and
Still doubling every thirty-five years, what we
innocently call our leadership
Turns family planning into a bad phrase;

If 400 million and more are still strangers to basic
essentials in life
An equal number effectively illiterate, and
A girl child still an object of rejection;

If our water table is beginning to get lower than oil,
Our rivulets and canals desiccated,
Our seas, rivers and brooks saturated with refuse
and effluents;

If open sewage in our midst froths pink, blue and
green,
With such blatant chemical pollution a rule rather than
exception, and
Our reaction to these sights at best phlegmatic;

If half our country still performs its morning ablutions
under the open skies, and
We are blissful being the world's largest open-air
lavatory, with
Basic hygiene and human dignity nobody's concern;

If elephants and rhinos, leopards and tigers are fast
disappearing,
Our mountains turning naked and barren with
denudation,
Forests disappearing rapidly under the onslaught of
deforestation;

If cows, dogs, donkeys, horses, even camels can roam
the busiest of streets,
With us incapable of arriving at a collective solution to
the problem, and
In the name of compassion, subject the poor animals
to the worst indignities;

If our national monuments are in a state of abject neglect,
Even a Taj Mahal stands upon a pile of a town's refuse
and indifference, with
Tourism a mere caricature of its potential;

If our public transport is perennially choking,
Our hospital lobbies resemble railway platforms, and
Our cities, towns and villages a vast compost heap;

If our railway stations and drainage pipes are
dwellings to zillions,
Sidewalks, if there, unavailable to pedestrians, and
Our traffic signals obeyed more in infraction than
compliance;

If our children are interviewed and waitlisted for
nursery admission,
A Class XII child with ninety per cent does not make it
to the nearest college, and
IITs, et al. brimming with 2,00,000 applications and
more for a handful of seats;

If we have to bribe a babu to pay our land taxes, and
We can get a 'RTO licence to kill' without a
driving test, with
Corruption in a government department a rule,
not exception;

If our bureaucracy is not a service but power centre,
and the system so corrupt that
85 per cent leakage in intended fundings nationally
acceptable, with
Local administration in cities, towns and villages but a
mere parody;

If a weak rupee is our best ticket to exports,
Quality, scale and punctuality at best secondary
concerns, and
Basic R&D still beyond the horizon;

If it takes three to mow a lawn, and we still
Erect buildings loading bricks on the heads
of our women, with
Our pace of change and productivity among the
slowest and lowest in the world;

If petitions are piled sky-high in every court
of the and, with
Justice nearly impossible to find in one's lifetime
(if then), and
Our dehumanized jails overflowing even as crime rates
continue to soar;

If Shanghai alone surpasses Indian's total exports three
times over, and
India's total port capacity by about the same margin, and
India's total foreign direct investment over ten times;

If, as a people, we have lost our sensitivity to the
misery and mediocrity around us, and
The only value system we can pass on to the next
generation is that of
Cynicism, opportunism, and corruption;

If our standards of satisfaction and excellence lie lower
than the soles of our feet, and
We are not filled with a sense of shame
At the gap between our rightful place in the world and
the present one;

Surely it's time to introspect collectively?

Are we, as believed by many, the worst self-bashers in the
world? My answer to that would be, 'We don't bash ourselves
hard enough.' Not seriously, at any rate. If we did, we would
also mend our actions collectively as a people. We would self-
regulate ourselves a spot more. We would be less deceitful in
our actions. We would be a tad more action-oriented. Our
problem is we confuse words for actions. Words come easily to
us. Action comes harder. We are long on petitions and affidavits,
short on delivery of justice. Our leaders are long on promises and
speeches, short on delivery; our teachers long on lectures, short

on research; our press long on reports, short on investigations; our products long on advertisements, short on quality.

We are ever ready to blame anyone but ourselves for our collective plight. For instance, we are always pointing fingers at the erratic traffic. Yet, I have never come across one who called himself a lousy driver. We drive with high beam, we honk endlessly, we jump red lights or ignore zebra crossings, we overtake from the left or speed across a one-way street—but we hardly see ourselves as defectors. This is not to say that every single Indian is a defector. There are those who are, by every reckoning, cooperators. But they are so few in number that they are unable to transport the country into a higher state of equilibrium. The number of defectors that typifies the country is so huge that it makes that minority of cooperators largely ineffective, or at any rate prevents the country from reaching its potential.

Not long ago a CEO of a large software company came forward to donate 1000 luggage trollies to a certain airport. The airport manager not only rejected the offer, but also behaved rudely with the CEO. Why would a reasonable official rebuff such an offer? You cannot fathom the reason unless you think like a typical Indian babu. If the manager were to accept such an offer, how could he float his annual tenders, which assure him an annuity of income? Naturally, he rejected the offer. Whoever said you shouldn't look a gift horse in the mouth obviously wasn't an Indian!

In another instance, a city pizza outlet franchisee of a national chain offered to place PVC garbage bins along the street where the outlet was located. His offer was refused as the municipal official thought having garbage bins would make litter on the street more conspicuous as people tend to throw the garbage around the bin rather than inside it. Having no bins, on the other hand, would diffuse the garbage over a larger area and hence make it less conspicuous!

Once when I tried to organize an event with about 300 school children and an equal number of employees of the organization I was heading, to clean up a prominent public park, the local authorities were reluctant to allow the event since that implied a formal acknowledgement that the park was dirty! It took considerable people-skills and media management to make the event happen.

In yet another instance, a colleague was sharing a public dais with a celebrated city police chief. Impressed by the latter's apparent angst at the city's traffic conditions, he offered to sponsor all traffic-discipline oriented hoardings in the city and left his card. When the cop did not call, my colleague tried to reach the officer but to no avail. Nor did the super-cop ever return the call, despite his office being repeatedly told about the purpose of the call.

Our corruption is so unique that we must be the only country in the world where even giving away money can involve graft! Why else would we need to grease the palm of the officials in the land registration offices?

The problem with citing these instances is that they tend to reinforce the inertia of the defectors with new-found justification for their defection. The usual reaction they elicit is, 'See, I told you there is no profit in being a cooperator in a country full of despicable defectors.' Each person aligns with the minority of cooperators, creating the illusion that the majority of defectors are some kind of aliens! We forget that it is the majority that typifies us and not the minority. We forget that the way we think is the way everyone thinks; that it is for us to be resolute with our cooperation. We forget that in this business of prisoner's dilemma, there is no second guessing what the other might do; it is what one must do oneself, one's own dharma—the absolute path of truth—that counts, and leads to the larger good of all.

Let me end this book with an apology to Rabindranath Tagore as I rewrite his most inspiring poem, 'Where the Mind Is without Fear', as 'Where the Neighbourhood Is without Filth':

Where the neighbourhood is without filth and the
    queues short and smooth;
Where civil service is corruption-free;
Where the towns have not been broken up into
    fragments by narrow potholed streets;
Where justice is given out quickly from the profundity
    of the courts;
Where a tireless work force stretches its arms towards
    perfection;
Where the clear stream from the mountains has not
    lost its way into contaminated rivers of dead water;
Where the economy is led forward by thee into a rate
    of growth higher than six per cent (real)—
Into that heaven of liberalization, my Father, let my
    country awake.

Yes, Rats Are Utility Maximizers

That lemming-like investors may well be utility maximizers, and hence rational, was reinforced when certain laboratory experiments found rats to be surprisingly rational in the sense assumed by finance theory. In a laboratory, rats were made to scurry through a series of parallel paths to get to their food. On each path, the rodents could expect to receive a certain quantum of food that was a random variable. In other words, on a given path, over several runs, a rat might expect to find on an average, say, 10 grams of food at the end of the run, while in any one run the amount of food could be more than or less than 10 grams. This is not unlike an investor on an average expecting to earn, say, 10 per cent annual return on a security, though in any given year the return may be more or less than 10 per cent.

Different paths had different expected quantum of food. For example, on path one, on an average, the rat could expect to find 10 grams of food; on path two, an average of 15 grams of food; on path three an average of 20 grams and so on, though on any one run, the quantum of food could vary from the average. However, there is never a free lunch. Not even for darting laboratory mice. Each pathway had a certain voltage of electric shock that the rodent had to endure if it wanted to reach the food at the other end. Before long, the rats showed behaviour that clearly indicated that for the same level of expected quantum of food at the other end, they preferred the route with lower voltage of shock; for a given voltage of shock, they preferred the path that held higher expected quantum of food; and finally for every unit of increased shock (say from 10 to 11 volts) they took the path that promised at least the same increase in the expected quantum of food as the previous unit of voltage increase entailed (that is, from 9 to 10 volts). In short, the rodents were perfect utility maximizers or perfectly rational. They knew what was best for them. There is then no reason to believe that human beings, a far more evolved species, should be any less rational.[1]

Pseudo Dilemmas

A few years ago, a law teacher came across a student who was willing to learn but was unable to pay the necessary fees.

The student struck a deal with the teacher saying, 'I will pay you your fee the day I win my first case in the court.'

The teacher agreed and proceeded with the law course.

Several months after the course the teacher started pressing the student to pay up the fee. The student reminded him that he was yet to win his first case and thus kept postponing the payment.

Fed up with this, the teacher decided to sue the student in the court of law and both of them decided to argue the case for themselves.

The teacher put forward his argument saying, 'If I win this case, as per the court of law, the student has to pay me as the case is about his non-payment of dues. And if I lose the case, student will still pay me because he would have won his first case. So either way I will have to get the money.'

The student, no less brilliant, argued saying, 'If I win the case, as per the court of law, I don't have to pay anything to the teacher as the case is about my non-payment of dues. And if I lose the case, I don't have to pay him because I haven't won my first case yet. So either way, I am not going to pay the teacher anything!'

WHAT ARE PSEUDO DILEMMAS?

To understand the significance of prisoner's dilemma (PD) better, it may be useful to consider some alternative 'dilemmas' that mimic prisoner's dilemma closely. First, let us recall from Chapter 4 that for prisoner's dilemma to hold, two conditions must hold, namely:

1) $T > R > P > S$, and
2) $(T+S)/2 < R$

where T, R, P and S are temptation, reward, punishment and sucker's payoff respectively.

We may recall that the first condition merely ensured that no matter what one did it was better for the other to defect. The second condition ensured that even if two players locked themselves into an arrangement where one month one defected and the other cooperated and the next month they switched roles, thus alternating roles forever, neither would do better. In fact, both would do worse than if they were both cooperating every month.

Now, consider a twist to the prisoner's dilemma, which we shall refer to as the pseudo prisoner's dilemma (PPD), whose payoff matrix is as shown in Figure A.1. In PPD, if you squeal when the accomplice does not, you walk free while the sucker gets three years instead of five as in the original prisoner's dilemma.

		You	
		Do Not Squeal	Squeal
I	Do Not Squeal	(−2, −2)	(−3, 0)
	Squeal	(0, −3)	(−4, −4)

Figure A.1 The Pseudo Prisoner's Dilemma Payoff Matrix

In the above payoff matrix of PPD, neither of the above two conditions for prisoner's dilemma is satisfied:

T = 0, R = −2, P = −4 and S = −3, so that
1) T > R > P < S, and
2) (T+S)/2 > R

Now why should that make any difference to the dilemma the prisoners face? At first glance, the situation seems to be no different from before, except that in this case the sucker's payoff is improved from five years behind the slammer to only three. Is it still better for you to squeal (that is, defect) no matter what I do? Of course, we are assuming once again that our only interest is to minimize the jail term for ourselves. No other sentiment is at work.

Suppose I squeal, what is your best course of action? It is obvious that if you squeal as well, we both get four years each. On the other hand if you do not squeal, you get away with only three years. So as one who is out only to minimize the sentence for oneself, it is in your interest not to squeal, given I have squealed. On the other hand, what if I do not squeal? If I have not squealed, it is in your interest to squeal, since that enables you to walk away without any prison sentence. So there is no unique course of action that guides you, unlike in the PD situation, where whatever I did, it was better for you to squeal. Of course the same symmetric reasoning holds for me as well. When faced with this one-time dilemma, you may as well toss a coin and decide whether you should squeal or not, based on whether you got a head or a tail, since you have no way of knowing whether or not I am going to squeal. And by symmetry, the same holds for me! Adopting this strategy, since each of the four scenarios (S–S, S–DS, DS–S, and DS–DS) is equally likely, our expected prison sentence will be 2.25 years [(2+3+0+4)/4] or [(T+R+P+S)/2]. May be a tad worse than getting away with two years each if both of us chose not to squeal but certainly not terribly worse considering the strategy of tossing a coin ensures that 25 per cent of the times you may get away scotfree and another 25 per cent of the times, you will get two years—the same as you will get for doing the 'right thing', that is, not squealing on each other (a DS–DS transaction).

This version of dilemma shows an added dimension when we consider an iterative situation with the following payoff matrix (Figure A.2), which is obtained by adding four to each number in Figure A.1.

		You	
		Cooperate (C)	Defect (D)
I	Cooperate (C)	(2, 2)	(1, 4)
	Defect (D)	(4, 1)	(0, 0)

Figure A.2 The Payoff Matrix for a Pseudo PD-Like Iterative Trade Agreement

Let us consider the goat and cheque trade agreement discussed in Chapter 3, with a payoff matrix as indicated in Figure A.2. It will be obvious to both of us within a few transactions that it is mutually beneficial for us to tacitly get locked into an arrangement where one month I defect and you cooperate, and the next month I cooperate and you defect, so that on an average our payoff is 2.5 each $[(1+4)/2$ or $(T+S)/2)]$ instead of mere 2 each if we both cooperate. This strategy, arising from the violation of the second necessary condition of prisoner's dilemma, proves superior to tossing a coin every time to decide whether to cooperate or defect. It can be easily seen that if both of us tossed a coin every time to decide whether to cooperate or defect, all the four scenarios (namely C–C, D–C, C–D and D–D) are equally likely, so that we would earn an average of only 1.75 points each per transaction!

WOLF'S DILEMMA

Here is yet another variation that departs from prisoner's dilemma, called Wolf's Dilemma. Consider the payoff matrix in Figure A.3. In this case:

1) $T > R > P > S$, and
2) $(T+S)/2 > R$

In other words, the first condition of prisoner's dilemma is satisfied, but the second condition is not. Clearly, the incentive to defect is high and, in a one-time play, the 'logical' reasoning invariably leads to D–D kind of decision. However, in case of an iterative situation as in PPD, Wolf's Dilemma also leads to a situation where both of us soon learn that we are better off getting locked into an arrangement where one month I defect and you cooperate and the next month I cooperate and you defect, so that our average payoff is a series of 25 points instead of a mere 5 each time when we both cooperate. This is a situation akin to a cartel-like arrangement in business. I am sure you will want to work it out for yourself!

		You	
		Cooperate (C)	Defect (D)
I	Cooperate (C)	(5, 5)	(0, 50)
	Defect (D)	(50, 0)	(1, 1)

Figure A.3 The Payoff Matrix for One-time Wolf's Dilemma

ENDNOTES

Prologue

[1] Douglas Hofstadter. Prisoner's dilemma, computer tournaments and the evolution of cooperation. *Scientific American* June 1983.

Chapter 1: Why Are We the Way We Are?

[1] I am aware that the old Hindu growth rate of 2 per cent has been replaced by what we proudly call as a 7 per cent growth rate today. But we conveniently forget that our population growth rate is a vigorous 2 per cent, so that the net real growth rate today is only about 5 per cent. But even this increase in productivity from 2 per cent to 5 per cent in about half a century is in itself a display of the Hindu rate of growth (of productivity) in action, so that our per capita economic base is among the lowest in the world.

[2] Excerpted from my article 'The idiot savants of India', *The Economic Times* 31 October 2005.

[3] V.S. Naipaul. 1977. *India: A Wounded Civilization.* Picador.

Chapter 4: Iterative Prisoner's Dilemma and We the Squealers!

[1] In fact Axelrod was investigating whether cooperation could emerge out of competition. This chapter and chapters elsewhere borrow liberally from his findings.

[2] Hofstadter tells the story of this experiment delightfully in 'Prisoner's dilemma, computer tournaments and the evolution of cooperation', *Scientific American* (May 1983).

Chapter 5: Can Competition Lead to Cooperation?

[1] Excerpted from Robert Axelrod's *The Evolution of Cooperation,* where he applies the standard prisoner's dilemma framework to explain the First World War phenomenon.

[2] Amartya Sen. 1977. Rational fools: A critique of the behavioral foundations of economic theory. *Journal of Philosophy and Public Affairs* 6.

Chapter 6: Self-regulation, Fairness and Us

[1] Richard H .Thaler. 1994. *The Winner's Curse: Paradoxes and Anomalies of Economic Life.* Princeton University Press. p. 3.

[2] Daniel Kahneman, Jack L. Knetsch, and Richard H. Thaler. *Journal of Economic Perspectives* **5**(1): 193–206.

[3] Zahira denies filing affidavit in apex court. *Times of India* 4 January 2005.

Chapter 7: Are We the World's Biggest Free Riders?

[1] Hardin explains the Tragedy of the Commons [*Science,* 162 (1968)] along the following lines. Consider a pasture that can sustain only ten cows optimally. Ten cowherds, owning one cow each, graze their cows on this pasture to fatten them for maximum yield of milk. One of the cowherds is tempted to add one more cow to the pasture. While he figures that adding another cow may mean less fodder for each of the cows, and this may reduce the yield of milk per cow somewhat, he is tempted nevertheless to add a cow since the cost of the additional cow will be actually shared by the other nine cowherds as well. But what is smart thinking for our cowherd is smart thinking for other cowherds as well and each tries to exploit the pasture more and more by adding more cows. And before you know it, the pasture, the cows and the cowherds are all losers.

[2] Richard H .Thaler. 1994. *The Winner's Curse: Paradoxes and Anomalies of Economic Life.* Princeton University Press.

[3] Richard H. Thaler. 1988. The ultimatum game. *Journal of Economic Perspectives* 2: 195–206; Kim Oliver and Mark Walker. 1984. The free rider problem: Experimental evidence. *Public Choice* 43: 3–24; Issac R. Mark, James M. Walker and Susan H. Thomas. 1984. Divergent evidence on free riding: An experimental examination of possible explanations. *Public Choice* 43: 113–49; and Jack Hirshleifer. 1985. The expanding domain of economics. *American Economic Review* 75(6): 53–70.

[4] Leon Felkins. Examples of social dilemma. http://perspicuity.net/sd/sd-exam.html

[5] F. de Zwart. 1994. *The Bureaucratic Merry-go-round: Manipulating the Transfer of Indian Civil Servants.* Amsterdam University Press.

Chapter 9: Veerappan Dilemma: The Poser Answered

[1] The computation of the probability as 38 per cent is as follows:

For any one of the twenty aspirants, the probability that he will draw a specific predetermined number and hence write is $1/20$ and that he will not draw the predetermined number and hence not write is $19/20$.

Thus, the conditional probability that the other nineteen will not draw their predetermined numbers and hence not write, given that one of the aspirants will draw the predetermined number and hence write is:

$$\frac{1}{20}\left[\frac{19}{20}\right]^{9}$$

As there are twenty aspirants in all, the sum total of the probabilities that there will be only one aspirant who will end up drawing the predetermined number and none else is:

$$\frac{20}{20}\left[\frac{19}{20}\right]^{9} = \left[\frac{19}{20}\right]^{9} = 0.377 @ 38\%$$

[2] In the world of quantum physics, the ordinary laws of physics break down, as all events are governed by probabilities and not certainties. For example, when a radioactive atom disintegrates, it might decay, emitting an electron, or it might not, with a certain probability. Schrödinger, much like Einstein, did not believe that God plays dice, and in order to show the 'absurdness' of the quantum mechanical implications, conceived the following conceptual experiment.

Imagine a closed carton that contains a live cat and a vial of poison, in addition to some radioactive material, arranged in such a manner that if the radioactive decay occurs, it will smash the poison vial, killing the cat. Now if the experiment is so set that there is exactly 50:50 chance of radioactive decay (which it is possible to set) one could then say there is a 50:50 chance that the cat will be killed. If so, one could equally safely make a statement, even without looking inside the box, that the cat is both dead and alive, each possibility having a 50 per cent chance. So far so good.

But there our intuitive world ends. According to quantum mechanics, neither of the two possibilities for the decaying atom, and hence the cat whose life is linked to the decay, has any reality unless the decay (or the state of the cat) is observed. The atom has neither decayed nor not decayed, so that the cat is neither dead nor not dead, till we take a peek inside the box! Believers in quantum mechanics consider the cat to be in some kind of indeterminate limbo, neither dead nor alive, until you take a look inside the box!

Appendix 1

A colleague made a passing reference to this experiment to me several years ago (in the mid 1980s) and even though I have tried hard I have not been able to find the exact reference to this experiment. However, I suspect this to be the work of John Kagel.

Index

adharma, 144, 147
Aumann, Robert J., 22
Axelrod, Robert, 56–58, 60–62, 67, 73

behavioural economics, 17, 19-20, 22-23, 25, 29, 86
Best Bakery case, 102-03
Bhagavad Gita, 21, 140–48

competition, 25, 56-57, 65, 89
    cooperation and, 66–74
cooperate, 20, 36, 37, 40, 51, 59, 130, 145, 162-63
cooperation, 25, 31, 37, 55, 71, 86, 130, 144
    competition and, 66–74
corporate governance, 42, 72
corruption, 44–46, 76, 93
    free riding and, 106, 110, 112–14

Dabbawalas systems, 123

defect, 36-37, 47, 50–53, 57–61, 73, 104, 117, 123, 145, 147-48, 160–63
defection, 37, 47, 50-51, 54-55, 59–61, 72, 86, 92, 104, 122-23, 129–31, 144, 155
dharma, 21, 144, 147-48
Dresher, Melvin, 33

Einstein, Albert, 144, 156

fairness, 20, 52, 73
    self-regulation, 85-86
    trust, 85-86
fatalism, 43–46
fear, 110-11
Felkins, Leon, 112
finance theory, 25-26, 86, 157
Flood, Merill, 33
foreign direct investment, 68
foreign universities in India, 69-70
forgetting, 59
forgiving, 59, 61

free ride/riding, 20, 30, 104, 106
    corruption and, 106, 110,
    112–14
    experiments, 106–08
    self-regulation and, 112
free riders, 105–14

gentleman strategy and
    Axelrod's experiment, 56–58
    iterative prisoner's dilemma,
    49–65
greed, 110-11

Hardin, Garrett, 106
Herzberg, Frederick, 77
Hindu fatalism, 13
Hindu growth rate, 13, 15
Hofstadter, Douglas, 2, 24, 37, 85

Indianness, canons of, 16-17,
    19-20
intelligence and rationality, 22–31
iterative prisoner's dilemma, 20,
    48–65, 72-73, 131
    gentleman strategy and, 49–65

Kahneman, Daniel, 25, 29, 87, 89
karmayogi, 145
Knetsch, 87
Krishna, Suresh, 70
Krishna, T.S., 70-71

live and let live policy, 66-67, 70
Luring Lottery, 2

massive retaliation, 53–55, 60
massive retaliators, 56, 63
Morgenstern, Oskar, 24

Naipaul, V.S., 10-11, 15, 19
name-change companies, 72-73
Nash, John, 24
Nathan, S.R., 76
Neumann, John von, 24
Never Again strategy, 53-54,
    59-60, 63-64
niceness, 61
Niemöller, Martin, 75
Nisbett, Richard, 11-12

odd-ball systems, 123-24

prisoner's dilemma, 20, 32–48,
    143–47, 156, 160
    exporters and, 38-39
    joint ventures and, 40-41
    like trade agreement, 36
    one-time, 33–35, 48
    payoff matrix, 34, 36, 50
pseudo dilemmas, 65, 159–63
punishment, 37-38, 101, 160

Rappaport, Alfred, 57, 61
rational fools, 70
rationality and intelligence, 22–31
return(s), 25
reward, 37, 41-42, 50, 60, 71, 160
risk, 25-26, 29, 80
Root, Hilton L., 113

Rubinstein, Ariel, 93

Schelling, Thomas C., 22
Scientific American, 24
selfishness, 25, 27, 31, 74, 147
self-regulation, 20, 75–114, 131
    fairness and trust, 85-86
    free riding and, 112
    lack of, 79
    public aesthetics and, 78
    public hygiene and, 75–77
Sen, Amartya, 99
Shrödinger's cat, 135-36, 139
social responsibility, 72
Srinivas, M.N., 11
Stahl, Ingolf, 93
sucker's payoff, 37, 160-61
supreme selfishness, 33–35, 47, 51-52, 73
systems
    anatomy, 116–21
    chaos, 115–31
    following and implementation, 115-16

lack of standardization, 129-30
    loopholes, 130-31

Tagore, Rabindranath, 156
temptation, 37–39, 41-42, 50-51, 53, 56, 73, 117, 146-47, 160
Thaler, Richard, 25, 29, 81, 83, 87, 106-07, 111
Tit for Tat strategy, 57–65, 67, 147
    in everyday life, 63-64
    in political life, 64-65
Tit for Two Tats strategy, 62
Tragedy of the Commons, 106
Transparency International, 44
Tucker, Albert, 33
Tversky, Amos, 25, 29

utility maximizers, 25-26, 157-58

Veerappan dilemma, 1–5, 131–39, 147

weak self-regulation
    and weaker regulation, 79-80
Wolf's dilemma, 162-63